Mary de Young

Incest

An Annotated Bibliography

McFarland & Company, Inc., Publishers
Jefferson, N.C., and London

Library of Congress Cataloging in Publication Data

de Young, Mary, 1949–
  Incest : an annotated bibliography.

  Includes indexes.
  1. Incest — Bibliography.   2. Child molesting —
Bibliography.   I. Title.
Z7164.S42D4   1985   [HQ71]   016.3067′77   84-43226

ISBN 0-89950-142-7

Manufactured in the United States of America

McFarland   Box 611   Jefferson NC 28640

Dedicated to:

Barbara Crozier
Robin Smietanka
Patricia Woodall

...and to all the others who have spent
a worried moment wondering how
they could get their hands on a 1959 issue
of the Hiroshima Journal of Medical Sciences.

Table of Contents

Acknowledgments

The preparation of this book benefited from the assistance of several very helpful people. My thanks to Kim Hayslip for her wizardry at the typewriter keyboard and for her meticulous attention to detail. I would also like to thank Robin Smietanka for her willingness to share her wealth of knowledge about incest and for her challenging of my knowledge, even though those erudite exchanges between us usually took place late at night, or on weekend morning trips to the library, or in the halls outside of a courtroom just before a trial.

1
Introduction

If the number of published articles in professional journals reflects the larger society's interest in a social problem, then incest is indeed a topic on many people's minds. The last ten years have witnessed a dramatic increase in empirical research, documented case studies, and theoretical considerations which have produced a body of knowledge on incest that clearly transcends the murky and vaguely scintillating areas of erotica and perversion to which it previously had been relegated.

The purpose of this book is twofold: to present the published references on incest in a manner that demonstrates that they collectively represent a body of scientific knowledge; and to group these references in a fashion that will allow them to describe the dynamics of the various types of incest, the effects on the victims, and the characteristics of the participants. This annotated bibliography focuses on references published in professional journals and in books; while there is a great deal of attention paid to incest in popular magazines and in pamphlets and booklets produced by the various organizations and agencies across the country that specialize in the treatment and prevention of incest, those are not included in this book.

The definition of incest used in each reference is a matter of some importance, and care has been taken to focus on that for each of the studies that has been summarized. These definitions vary widely and as is discussed in Chapter 2, they also have an impact on estimates of the rate of occurrence of incest, the effects it has on the victims, and the intervention strategies required to resolve it. Similar attention has been focused on the settings in which the studies were conducted. Certainly those studies which use psychotherapy patients for subjects, as an example, are likely to find more mental illness in the subjects than in those studies which use students; or, as another example, those studies which have samples of court-referred cases are likely to document more aggression and general social dysfunction than those studies which use psychotherapy patients as subjects. In any type of behavioral and social science research those types of variables are important and that is no less true for incest research.

To call a thing by its precise name is the beginning of understanding. Incest refers to some kind of sexual activity between individuals who are in some fashion related to each other. Because one of the participants in this behavior is most often a child or adolescent, incest is clearly most often an act of child sexual abuse, yet it is not the only act that falls under the general rubric of child sexual abuse. Children are also sexually molested by strangers, by acquaintances, and by people intimately involved in their lives; they are exploited by child sex rings, prostitution, and pornography, and all of these behaviors constitute child sexual abuse. Some of the references in this book do not clearly distinguish between incest and other forms of child sexual abuse and use the terms in the generic sense, mixing samples of incest victims with molestation victims, or developing theoretical constructs around this behavior without thoroughly investigating the dynamics.

There is little question that the scientific body of knowledge on child sexual abuse in general would benefit greatly from studies that are more specific about the **type** of child sexual abuse being examined. While that is an area of concern for research, it also posed certain problems in the preparation of this book. Judgment had to be exercised as to whether some of the references on child sexual abuse contained enough specific data on incest to be included in this book. Those references for which the information on incest could not be easily culled from the data were eliminated; those for which that task could be accomplished were included. In deference to the dictum that to call a thing by its precise name is the beginning of understanding, the word "incest" as used in this book will refer to some type of sexual activity between individuals who are in some fashion related to each other; the term "child sexual abuse" will refer to other, nonincestuous forms of sexual molestation and exploitation.

Even the most carefully researched bibliography will overlook some references on the topic being examined, and this book is no exception. Any exclusions of references on incest are simply due to an oversight by the author who apologizes in advance to those researchers, theorists, and practitioners who have added to our knowledge about this behavior but are not included in this book. Similarly, the author assumes responsibility for any annotations that do not adequately reflect the content and quality of the reference, and offers the same apologies for any errors in judgment.

Finally, it is hoped that this book will be useful to any individual who wants to know more about incest. It is geared towards the busy clinicians and researchers who require an expedient way to have access to the professional literature on incest, and if it is in any way helpful in increasing their knowledge about this topic, the book's purpose will have been realized.

2

Definitions of Incest

Whether incest is defined as sexual intercourse, or as sexual contact, or even as attempted sexual contact, is not just a matter of semantics. The definitions of incest used in the various references in the professional literature have a great deal to do with estimates of its rate of occurrence, its effects on the victims, and the intervention strategies that may be required to resolve it. The lack of a standardized definition in incest research has contributed to inconsistent conclusions and an unhealthy amount of confusion among researchers, practitioners, and theorists.

Take as an example the effect that varying definitions have on the assessment of the rate of occurrence of incest. When incest is defined as sexual intercourse, a definition that is used in most of the earlier studies and in some of the more recent ones, then it is indeed a rare phenomenon from a statistical point of view. Early figures that estimate that incest occurs in only one out of a million families are generally based upon this definition of incest. When incest is defined as sexual contact, or even as attempted sexual contact, its estimated rate of occurrence ranges in the literature from one out of a hundred families, to one out of four.

The various definitions also predict, to some degree, the effects incest will have on the victims. A child who has experienced sexual intercourse is likely to be more traumatized by that act than a child who has experienced fondling. The act of intercourse, particularly on a young child, can also be physically traumatizing and the emotional impact that will have on the child is likely to be considerably greater as well.

Finally, the various definitions of incest also affect the intervention strategies necessary to effectively resolve the family problem. Most of the references in the literature to the nature of the incestuous family as a system would agree that a family in which the incest has not progressed beyond sexual contact may be more treatable, if all other

5

variables are held constant, than a family in which the incest involves sexual intercourse.

The definition of incest, then, is not just an exercise in semantics; it is, instead, a powerful tool for the estimation of the rate of occurrence, the effects on the victims, and the necessary intervention strategies. Yet the type of sexual behavior implied by the definition of incest is not the only important variable. The degree of relatedness between the perpetrator of the offense and the victim is another factor that must be carefully considered. Although it may have less of an impact on the predicted effects and on the necessary intervention strategies, the degree of relatedness between the participants is another important variable in estimating the rate of occurrence of incest. In a rapidly changing society where the dissolution of natural families is a common experience for millions of children, a definition of incest that only accommodates sexual behavior between blood relatives almost certainly will underestimate the number of children and adolescents who have been sexually victimized. Extending that definition of incest to include sexual behavior between people related by legal or social means will lead to a considerably higher estimate of the rate of occurrence.

One other factor in the various definitions of incest is also important. Some definitions only consider heterosexual activity in their considerations of incest. Incest may also be homosexual in nature, and choosing to ignore or deny that reality will once again affect estimates of the rate of occurrence, the effects of the incest on the victims, and the necessary intervention strategies.

A perusal of the incest literature leaves no doubt that wide-sweeping definitional reform is needed, and that research and theory would benefit greatly from a standardized definition of incest, as the following references suggest.

1. Bixler, R.H. "The Incest Controversy." **Psychological Reports,** 49(1): 267-283, August 1981.

The definition of incest must to some degree reflect biological, social and moral factors that complement the incest taboo. Those include: the theory of natural selection; the sexual preference continuum which places a premium on the moderate novelty of sexual partners; the capacity to recognize or suspect a relationship between consanguineous mating and defective offspring; the reduction of sexual competition; the moral repulsion attending incest behavior; and the fear of punishment for engaging in that behavior.

2. Bixler, R.H. "The Multiple Meanings of 'Incest.'" **Journal of Sex Research,** 19(2): 197–201, May 1983.

Studies on incest must specify the degree of relatedness between the participants; the age and sex of the participants; the type of sexual activity; the amount of willingness involved in the relationship; and whether the participants were associated intimately during prepubescence.

3. Mrazek, P.B. "Sexual Abuse of Children." **Journal of Child Psychology and Psychiatry,** 21(1): 91–95, January 1980.

A working clinical definition of incest must include: an explicit description of the nature of the sexual act, its frequency, and whether it was accompanied by violence or threats of violence; information about the age, developmental and intellectual levels of the participants; a description of the relationship between them; and an examination of the attitudes of the participants, the family members, and the prevailing culture.

3
Father-Daughter Incest

For most people the very word "incest" conjures up the image of a father engaged in a sexual relationship with his daughter. Subtleties of that impression may include differing perceptions of the father as alcoholic, or violent, or mentally ill; the daughter as a willing participant or as an unwilling victim; the family as economically deprived or chaotically disorganized; and the social forces impacting on the family as inhibiting overt incest or as encouraging it.

Indeed, all of these variables and many more have been examined in the scientific literature on paternal incest and themes emerge from the research when these individual elements are combined and filtered through the theoretical orientations of the authors. Some researchers, as an example, have a sociological perspective that stresses the impact of forces generally external to the family and over which the family has little, if any, control and which influence the etiology of incest. The characterological perspective, on the other hand, examines incest from the slant of mental illness or of individual differences, while the psychosocial perspective views incest as a product of family dysfunction and describes the family as an interdependent system that functions to encourage or to discourage the etiology of incest. In recent years a feminist perspective has appeared in the literature. This theoretical orientation sees incest as a product of a larger patriarchal society in which the subjugation and victimization of women and children is not only tolerated but is also encouraged.

Each of these theoretical perspectives has made a significant contribution to the understanding of the complexities of father-daughter incest. The importance of each may be weighed according to the extent its orientation is compatible with that of the reader, or its value may be determined by the extent to which it provides one more piece of knowledge that can be fit into the larger puzzle of paternal incest.

Sociological Perspective

Father-daughter incest as viewed through the sociological perspective is seen as arising from a combination of factors and forces that are for the most part external to the family. Low socioeconomic status, subcultural values, overcrowding, social isolation, among others, all have been examined as being possible antecedents and reinforcers of paternal incest.

Since so many of these factors and forces exist outside of the control of the family, research from the sociological perspective tends to de-emphasize the roles that individual family members play in the incest. Consequently, this perspective frequently omits data or even speculations about the possible effects that incest can have on the victims, or about the modalities needed for therapeutic intervention with incestuous families. To the extent that the family as a system is considered, it is frequently viewed as a victim of external forces although some suggestions as to the internal weaknesses that render these families vulnerable to social stress appear in some of the references. Presumably this theoretical orientation encourages social change in order to prevent incest although prevention strategies, per se, are rarely discussed in the literature that reflects the sociological perspective.

4. Julian, V. and Mohr, C. "Father-Daughter Incest: Profile of the Offender." **Victimology: An International Journal,** 4(4): 348-360, 1979.

Using the data base of the National Study on Child Neglect and Abuse Reporting Project, the authors examine 102 reported cases of paternal incest and compare these to a comparable number of cases of physical abuse reported to the project. Paternally incestuous families have more children, a higher average annual income, and a lower rate of unemployment than the physically abusive families. Family discord is also more prevalent with significantly higher rates of alcoholism, mental health problems, and spouse abuse reported. Perhaps because of these documented problems, paternally incestuous families are more likely to be referred to the social service and mental health agencies.

5. Kubo, S. "Researches and Studies on Incest in Japan." **Hiroshima Journal of Medical Sciences.** 8: 99-159, 1959.

Thirty-six incestuous families in Japan share rural isolation and rigid adherence to an economically, socially

and religiously created feudal family system which allows
incest to be regarded as praiseworthy conduct in those families
in which the mother has died or is incapacitated.

6. Riemer, S. "A Research Note on Incest." **American
Journal of Sociology,** 45: 566-575, 1940.

Referred for mandatory psychiatric treatment, fifty-
eight incestuous fathers have backgrounds of economic deprivation, physical and/or verbal violence within the family,
and an alcoholic parent. Most of the subjects had left home
at an early age, failing to complete their formal education,
and as adults had drifted from one low paying job to another.
Eventually replicating their own family background, they
married passive, ineffectual women with whom they developed
conflictual and violent relationships exacerbated by alcohol
abuse. They lived in economically deprived and overcrowded
conditions which afforded opportunities for incestuous behavior with their own children. The author acknowledges that
the life careers of the subjects do not constitute a cause
of incest, but that the probability of incest is increased
given the configuration of events in the lives of these men.

7. Scheurell, R.P. and Rinder, I.P. "Social Networks
and Deviance: A Study of Lower Class Incest, Wife Beating
and Non-Support Offenders." **Wisconsin Sociologist,** 19(2-3):
56-73, Spring 1973.

Ten incestuous fathers are compared to a comparable
number of wife abusers and non-support offenders. All three
groups have segregated patterns of conjugal role performance,
however the incestuous fathers demonstrate a greater disparity between their behavior and the role expectations of
the larger society. They are also significantly more socially
isolated with little access to social networks of peers and
of helping agencies.

8. Schultz, L.G. and Jones, P. "Sexual Abuse of Children:
Issues for Social Service and Health Professionals." **Child
Welfare,** 62(2): 99-108, March/April 1983.

To test the popular stereotype that incest is most
prevalent in rural and mountain geographical areas, the
authors surveyed 267 West Virginia students who had lived
in that state for at least a decade before the age of eighteen.
The results of a forced-choice questionnaire which elicited
information about the students' childhood sexual experiences
and their reactions to them suggest that city-reared females
may be more vulnerable to childhood sexual experiences,

and that since none of the rural-raised females had experienced incest as a child, the stereotype of rural, mountain
families as incest-prone has no basis in reality.

   9. Weinberg, S.K. **Incest Behavior.** New York: Citadel,
1955.

   A sample of 203 reported cases of incest, 159 of which
were paternal in nature, contains a larger portion of blacks
and foreign born whites than would be estimated on the
basis of the ethnic population of the state of Illinois in which
the study was conducted. Lower socioeconomic class families
are also overrepresented, with many of them experiencing
chronic unemployment, crowded living conditions, and isolation
from the network of social service agencies as well as severe
family disorganization which is demonstrated in intrafamilial
violence and a loose sex culture in which a general tolerance
of sexual activity and a lack of sexual privacy are common.

Characterological Perspective

   This theoretical orientation emphasizes the roles that
mental illness and individual differences play in paternal
incest. While the incestuous family as a system is usually
considered to be dysfunctional, this perspective emphasizes
the pathology of individual family members and how those
combine and interact to create strains and tensions within
the family system.

   The characterological perspective is also to some
extent a developmental approach. Hypothesizing that individual pathology is largely learned behavior, this orientation
tends to examine the personal histories of the members
of the incestuous family and speculates as to how each person
adapts to the other's deviance and how that accommodation,
in turn, can create a family environment that is conducive
to incest.

   Many of the studies in this perspective are written
by mental health professionals, therefore case study and
descriptive approaches are common, although experimental
research with control groups are beginning to emerge from
this theoretical orientation. An emphasis is also placed in
most of these studies on the early recognition of characterological indicators of incest, prompt intervention, and individual
and family treatment.

10. Anderson, L.M. and Shafer, G. "The Character-Disordered Family: A Community Treatment Model for Family Sexual Abuse." **American Journal of Orthopsychiatry,** 49(3): 436-445, July 1979.

An analogy between the sociopathic personality disorder and a character-disordered family is made by the authors on the basis of their study of sixty-two paternally incestuous families. Both demonstrate symptomatology that includes poor judgment, a failure to learn from past experiences, conflicts with authority figures, poor impulse control, manipulativeness, irresponsibility, narcissism, dependency conflicts, an inability to tolerate intimacy and little guilt and anxiety.

11. Cohen, T. "The Incestuous Family Revisited." **Social Casework,** 64(3): 154-161, March 1983.

The incestuous father is described as overinvested in his family, seeking to exert paternal control over family members. Because he comes from an emotionally deprived family, he identifies with his daughter and then through the incest gives her the attention and affection he had wanted as a child. The mother is passive and withdrawn having abdicated her role in the family. She tends to displace the ambivalence she has about her own mother onto her daughter and collusively encourages the incest to occur. The non-victimized siblings also have difficulty coping with the changes in roles and in communication that precede and accompany the incest.

12. Cormier, B.M.; Kennedy, M.; and Sangowicz, J. "Psychodynamics of Father-Daughter Incest." **Canadian Psychiatric Association Journal,** 7(5): 203-217, October 1962.

A sample of twenty-seven incarcerated or psychiatric hospitalized male incest offenders are of normal intelligence and are able to economically provide for their families. They also exploit their authoritative role in the family by developing controlling, jealous relationships with their daughters and by projecting blame onto them for behaving in a seductive fashion. Their wives are perceived by the subjects as hostile and rejecting, and their emotional and sexual withdrawal and the role reversal they affect with their daughters set the stage for the incest. Once the incest is disclosed, the fathers vehemently deny their role in the victimization and when they later acknowledge that the incest has taken place, they tend to project the blame for the act on their daughters.

13. de Young, M. "Incest Victims and Offenders: Myths and Realities." **Journal of Psychosocial Nursing and Mental Health Services,** 19(10): 37-39, October 1981.

Debunking some of the more persistent myths about paternal incest, the pathology of individual family members is described and speculations as to how each person accommodates to the others' deviance in incestuous families are offered.

14. de Young, M. **The Sexual Victimization of Children.** Jefferson, N.C.: McFarland, 1982.

The author defines incest as sexual intercourse, attempted sexual intercourse or sexual contact between two people too closely related to legally marry and examines fifty-five incestuous fathers, sixty paternal incest victims, and twelve nonparticipating family members. The fathers are patriarchal, frequently violent individuals who present a socially acceptable facade to the larger world. Unable to effectively parent, they are self-involved and dependent and develop conflictual relationships with their wives who abdicate their parenting role in order to cope with the tensions within the family. The nonvictimized siblings also experience tension within the family and frequently act out antisocially or in a self-defeating fashion. The study also focuses on the role the victim plays prior to, during and after the incest, and examines the effects incest has on the emotional and psychological development of the victim.

15. Herman, J.L. and Hirschman, L. "Families at Risk for Father-Daughter Incest." **American Journal of Psychiatry,** 138(7): 967-970, July 1981.

Forty adult women who had been incestuously abused in their childhood are compared to twenty adult women whose fathers had been sexually seductive in their childhood but who had not engaged in overt incest. Both groups describe the fathers as the dominant parent although the incestuous fathers are depicted as considerably more physically violent. More of the incest victims describe their mothers as ill or otherwise incapacitated during their childhood, and role reversals with the mothers as well as periodic separations from them are more often reported. Suicidal behavior, running away from home, substance abuse, and early pregnancy are more often reported from incest victims, leading the authors to conclude that overt incest victimization tends to prematurely foreclose the major developmental stages through which children must progress.

16. Kaufman, I.; Peck, A.L.; and Tagiuri, C.K. "The Family Constellation and Overt Incestuous Relations Between Father and Daughter." **American Journal of Orthopsychiatry,** 24(2): 266-277, 1954.

Eleven girls who had been incestuously victimized by their fathers show symptoms of anxiety, depression, guilt feelings and antisocial or self-defeating behaviors. Their mothers are passive, dependent women who had developed tense and unhappy relationships with their daughters before the incest occurred.

17. Lukianowicz, N. "Incest I: Paternal Incest; Incest II: Other Types of Incest." **British Journal of Psychiatry,** 120(556): 301-313, March 1972.

Most of the twenty-six paternal incest offenders in this Northern Ireland study are diagnosed as psychopathic, with strong sexual drives and weak impulse control. Of average intelligence, despite a poor ability to maintain employment, the subjects have strained, unhappy marriages with masochistic and frequently promiscuous wives. The children cope by acting out aggressively and sexually.

18. Magal, V. and Winnick, H.Z. "Role of Incest in Family Structure." **Israel Annals of Psychiatry and Related Disciplines,** 6: 173-189, 1963.

All of the five incestuous families in treatment in a psychiatric facility in Israel are dysfunctional. Two of the fathers are psychotic and the remainder are largely incompetent and frequently abusive. The mothers are fearful and passive, withdrawing from their families and affecting role reversals with their daughters. Due to their strong needs for affection and attention, the victimized daughters are also likely to be sexually abused by their brothers.

19. Maisch, H. **Incest.** New York: Stein and Day, 1972.

The fathers of the sixty-eight paternally incestuous families in this court-referred West Germany sample exercise patriarchal control over the family and create through their own pathology a disturbed marriage relationship with their weak, passive and frequently incapacitated wives. The daughters are fearful of disclosing the incest and often engage in antisocial behavior outside of the family.

20. Meiselman, K.C. **Incest: A Psychological Study of Causes and Effects with Treatment Recommendations.** San Francisco: Jossey-Bass, 1978.

Defining incest as a very definite sexual approach involving successful or unsuccessful attempts at exposure, genital fondling, oral-genital contact, and/or vaginal or anal intercourse with relatives by blood, marriage or adoption, fifty-eight incest victims, thirty-seven of whom had been victimized by their fathers, are compared to a control group of one hundred psychotherapy patients who have not reported a history of incest victimization. Incestuous fathers are described by their daughters as replicating within their families the emotional deprivation and abuse they had experienced as children. The mothers are depicted as having a vested interest in denying that the incest has taken place and the siblings of the victim are also adversely affected by the family pathology. The study focuses on the effects that incest can have on the victims.

21. Renshaw, D.C. **Incest: Understanding and Treatment.** Boston: Little, Brown and Company, 1982.

A descriptive approach to incest, this study focuses on the individual pathology of members of the incestuous family.

22. Spencer, J. "Father-Daughter Incest: A Clinical View from the Corrections Field." **Child Welfare**, 57(9): 581-589, November 1981.

Incestuous fathers have paranoic personalities with rigid defenses, an authoritarian and frequently abusive style of interacting, religious fanaticism and alcohol abuse. Insecure about their masculinity, they marry weak, dependent women who cannot protect their children from abuse and are unlikely to believe their children when the incest is disclosed. The victims, in turn, often engage in self-destructive behaviors such as running away from home, substance abuse and suicide attempts.

Psychosocial Perspective

This perspective acknowledges both the sociological and characterological aspects of paternal incest, and it focuses on the frequently subtle and at times nearly imperceptible changes that occur in incestuous families. Role reversals, shifts in power, deteriorating communication patterns, and blurred generational boundaries are common in these families and are symptoms of the dysfunctional nature of the system.

The role that collusion plays in incest is also stressed in this theoretical orientation. Although each family member may not be cognizant that overt incest is actually occurring, each participates in the subtle changes within the family that allow the incest to begin in the first place, reinforce its continuation over time, and keep its secret from the outside world.

23. de Young, M. "Promises, Threats and Lies: Keeping Incest Secret." **Journal of Humanics,** 9(1): 61-71, May 1981.

An incestuous father places a great deal of pressure on his daughter to keep the incest secret. This reference examines the nature of that pressure, the effects it has on the victims, and the role that family members may play in colluding to maintain the secret.

24. Eist, H.I. and Mandel, A.U. "Family Treatment of Ongoing Incest Behavior." **Family Process,** 7(2): 216-232, September 1968.

Each of the members of a family referred for treatment by the authors was secretive and dishonest about the incest and the family as a system had no clear sense of generational boundaries and appropriate family roles.

25. Gordon, L. and O'Keefe, P. "Incest as a Form of Family Violence: Evidence from Historical Case Records." **Journal of Marriage and the Family,** 46(1): 27-34, February 1984.

Fifty cases of incest contained in the records of social service agencies in Boston between 1880 and 1960 are compared to cases of physical abuse on record. Incestuous families are characterized by domineering, controlling fathers and weak, incapacitated mothers. Since the incestuous father historically has been less likely to be living in the home when the incest occurs, the incestuous act must be a coldly calculated and carefully strategized crime of opportunity with which the mothers and siblings collude. No evidence from historical case records prove that incestuous families are under more external stress than are families in which physical abuse had taken place.

26. Gutheil, T.G. and Avery, N.C. "Multiple Overt Incest as Family Defense Against Loss." **Family Process,** 16(1): 105-116, March 1977.

Separation anxiety develops in families that agree on four basic issues: that the dissolution of the family would be traumatic; that allegiance to the parents is paramount; that emotional ties inevitably will be severed with children who leave the family; and that the world outside of the family is threatening and dangerous. Once that anxiety has been created, the family is motivated to remain intact even when it is largely dysfunctional and filled with tension and unhappiness. Incest as an overt act defends against this separation anxiety, keeping the family intact when the skills and strengths of the individual family members have been depleted. Incest accomplishes this function by allowing the mother to vicariously experience the acting out of her own unresolved Oedipal wishes; by relieving the sexual pressure between the parents; and by improving the marital relationship since the father's incestuous behavior creates guilt feelings for which he may overcompensate by behaving more affection-ately with his wife. One extensive case study is presented to illustrate this theory.

27. Heims, L.W. and Kaufman, I. "Variations on a Theme of Incest." **American Journal of Orthopsychiatry,** 33(2): 311-312, 1963.
Twenty emotionally disturbed girls who are in treatment for incest-related problems come from one of four different types of incestuous families. In the family in which overt incest occurs, there is a role reversal between the daughter and her mother, and an exploitation by the father of his role in the family. In the family in which overt incest occurs with the knowledge of all of the children, although all are not victimized, the same family dynamics occur. Incest fantasies are shared although never acted upon in some families which tend to exhibit significant role confusion. Finally, in the family in which incestuous wishes are strongly defended against, power shifts and role reversals are common.

28. Janas, C. "Family Violence and Child Sexual Abuse." **Medical Hypoanalysis,** 4(2): 68-76, April 1983.
There are several stages of an incestuous act: engage-ment, sexual interaction, secrecy, disclosure, and suppression. Each stage requires the family's unconscious reinforcement and the movement from one stage to another as the incest progresses over time is dependent upon concomitant changes in family roles, power structure, and communication patterns.

29. Johnson, M.S. "Recognizing the Incestuous Family." **Journal of the National Medical Association,** 75(8): 757-761, 1983.

Addressing family physicians, the author discusses the behavioral and medical clues to incest victimization that may be gleaned from a thorough family study of the patient.

30. Justice, B. and Justice, R. **The Broken Taboo.** New York: Human Sciences Press, 1979.

Sudden and frequent stresses on the 112 incestuous families in this study have a deleterious effect on the integrity of family roles, generational boundaries, and communication patterns, thereby creating a family environment conducive to incest.

31. Lustig, N.; Dresser, J.W.; Spellman, S.W.; and Murray, T.B. "Incest: A Family Group Survival Pattern." **Archives of General Psychology,** 14(1): 31-40, January 1966.

The incestuous family is a dysfunctional family characterized by a role reversal between the mother and the daughter; a sexual imcompatibility between the parents; a father who is unwilling to go outside of the family for gratification of his sexual needs; shared family fears of abandonment and dissolution; and a mother who plays a collusive role in the incest. Since this dysfunctional family fears separation, incest becomes an attempt to keep the family together by meeting the parents' dependency needs and by allowing the expression of revenge by the daughter against her mother for the rejection she has experienced. Six case studies are presented to illustrate this theory.

32. MacFarlane, K. and Korbin, J. "Confronting the Incest Secret Long After the Fact: A Family Study of Multiple Victimization with Strategies for Intervention." **Child Abuse and Neglect,** 7(2): 225-237, 1983.

In one extended family used as a case example, all eleven females in one generation have been incestuously victimized by two male relatives. The incest was a closely guarded secret for twenty years due to the collusion of the individual family members. Intervention strategies for families in which multiple victimization has taken place are discussed.

33. Machota, P.; Pittman, F.S.; and Flomenhaft, K. "Incest as a Family Affair." **Family Process,** 6: 98-116, 1967.

Three paternally incestuous families illustrate the theory that incest serves a function within severely disorganized families by freezing role relationships and preserving them from any change that would stress the system. The roles of nonparticipating family members are described as collusive in nature and as essential for the initiation and the continuation of the incest.

34. Messer, A.A. "The Phaedra Complex." **Archives of General Psychiatry,** 21(2): 213-218, August 1969.

In Greek mythology, Phaedra, the wife of Theseus, falls tragically in love with her stepson. This mythological construct is used to describe the potential sexual attraction between members of a family in which a stepparent has been introduced. The family romance, in which the child flirts with the parent of the opposite sex, is a normal part of child development but in stepfamilies the relaxation of the incest taboo may result in the unhealthy sexualization of this flirtation. Techniques for reinforcing the incest taboo in stepfamilies include an equal participation in discipline by both the natural parent and the stepparent; the use of the words "mom" and "dad" by the children; the enhancement of a romantic bond between the parents so that the children are exposed to a model of adult sexuality within acceptable role constraints; and the adoption of stepchildren by the stepparent.

35. Raphling, D.L.; Carpenter, B.L.; and Davis, A. "Incest: A Geneological Study." **Archives of General Psychiatry,** 16(4): 505-511, April 1967.

The social learning model of incest is illustrated by a case study of a family in which incest has occurred in three generations.

36. Rhinehart, J.W. "Genesis of Overt Incest." **Comprehensive Psychiatry,** 2(6): 338-349, December 1961.

The social learning model of incest is illustrated by four case studies of families in which incest has occurred in more than one generation.

37. Rosenfeld, A.A. "Sexual Misuse and the Family." **Victimology: An International Journal,** 2(2): 226-235, Summer 1977.

Incest represents the extreme and abhorrent end of a continuum of sexual behavior within the family. At the other extreme lies normal, healthy sexual expression within the family that is characterized by parents who do not attempt to get their genital-sexual needs met by their children; no seduction or overstimulation of the child; an ability to tolerate social and personal intimacy between the parents and the children without sexual involvement; a culturally acceptable degree of warmth and affection without discomfort or inhibition, or a rejection of the cultural norms that deny that experience; adequate privacy for all family members; honest sexual information given by the parents to the children; a willingness and ability to change and adapt in order to accommodate the child's developmental stages; consistent child-rearing techniques; and a good, comfortable relationship between the parents and the children.

38. Thorman, G. **Incestuous Families.** Springfield, Illinois: Charles C. Thomas, Publisher, 1983.

Case studies illustrate the dynamics of the incestuous family which are characterized by a lack of a strong coalition between the parents; a role reversal between the mother and the daughter; an unequal distribution of power between the parents; conflict resolution through scapegoating; confused communication; social isolation; an inability to tolerate stress; and an absence of emotional support and autonomy.

39. Weich, M.J. "The Terms 'Mother' and 'Father' as a Defence Against Incest." **Journal of the American Psychoanalytic Association,** 16(4): 783-791, 1968.

There is an increased likelihood of incest in stepfamilies. The terms "mother" and "father" to designate the natural parent and the stepparent reinforce the incest taboo and decrease the likelihood of overt incest.

Feminist Perspective

Feminism has brought a new perspective on paternal incest. The patriarchy of the father, so often alluded to in the references in the characterological and psychosocial perspectives, is focused upon as the primary cause of incest. Recognizing that many cultural, political and religious influences legitimatize the patriarchal rule of the father, the feminists tend to place paternal incest within a larger social context that has been conducive to the sexual victimization of children.

The subjugation and victimization of women and children is considered to be a product of patriarchy. References in the literature to collusive mothers and seductive daughters are often cited by these researchers as examples of how traditional incest research has so often displaced the blame on the victim and in so doing at least partially exonerates the offending father for his behavior.

Feminism asserts that incest prevention lies not only in comprehensive social, political and religious changes, but also in the strengthening of maternal roles and the empowering of women and children.

40. Breines, W. and Gordon, L. "The New Scholarship on Family Violence." **Signs**, 8(3): 490-553, Spring 1983.

Child abuse, wife beating and incest are all forms of family violence. Feminist writers and researchers are credited for bringing long overlooked facts about incest to the attention of laypersons and professionals.

41. Brownmiller, S. **Against Our Will.** New York: Simon and Schuster, 1975.

This feminist analysis of rape also discusses the incestuous abuse of children. In a patriarchal society the systematic dehumanization of women and children has created cultural support for their victimization and in that way, rape differs little from incest.

42. Herman, J.L. and Hirschman, L. "Father-Daughter Incest." **Journal of Women in Culture and Society**, 2(4): 735-756, 1977.

The seduction of the daughter by the father is an act inherent within a patriarchal society, therefore the greater the degree of male supremacy in any culture, the greater the prevalence of paternal incest. Fifteen victims in psychotherapy for incest-related problems describe the patriarchal structure of their families and the effects that incest has had on them.

43. Herman, J.L. "Father-Daughter Incest." **Professional Psychology**, 12(1): 76-80, 1981.

Paternally incestuous families are characterized by pathologically exaggerated patriarchal norms that stress paternal dominance, maternal disability, and the imposition of the mothering role on the oldest daughter. Measures to improve the general status of women in society and to strengthen the role of mothers in families are presented as prevention strategies.

44. Herman, J.L. **Father-Daughter Incest.** Cambridge, Massachusetts: Harvard University Press, 1981.

Forty adult women in psychotherapy for incest-related problems are compared to twenty psychotherapy clients

who do not report a history of incest victimization. A feminist
analysis of their cases challenges traditional psychoanalytic
theory that relegates accusations of incest victimization
to the fantasies of children; the male dominated social structure that has a vested interest in suppressing information
about the prevalence and effects of incest; and the legal
system that treats with skepticism any female who complains
of having been sexually victimized.

45. Rush, F. **The Best Kept Secret.** Englewood Cliffs,
New Jersey: Prentice-Hall, 1980.
    Social, religious and political patterns throughout
history have been conducive to the sexual exploitation and
victimization of children. A feminist analysis is used to
emphasize the influence of patriarchy in the formation of
attitudes, values and practices that have systematically
devalued women and children and have created opportunities
for their victimization.

46. Westerlund, E. "Counseling Women with Histories
of Incest." **Women and Therapy,** 2(4): 17-31, Winter 1983.
    A patriarchal society which denies men access to their
feelings and prevents them from assuming equal child care
responsibilities with women allows them to exercise certain
rights over women and children and refuses to hold them
fully accountable for their behavior. Men are more likely
to see children in a dehumanized fashion, as objects that
can be manipulated, used and abused, a perception that
is reinforced by a society which devalues both women and
children because of their decreased ability to contribute
economically to the social order.

General Perspectives

    Other references to the paternally incestuous family
are more difficult to categorize. Some review the literature
in general while others present case material to illustrate
some special aspect of the incestuous family.

47. Bagley, C. "Incest Behavior and the Incest Taboo."
Social Problems, 16(4): 505-519, Spring 1969.
    Fifty published articles on incest are reviewed and
from them, five types of incest are proposed. Functional
incest develops out of a patriarchal family structure that
is also characterized by social isolation and economic depriva-

tion and is an act that serves to keep the family together. Accidental incest occurs in communities that are socially disorganized and significantly overcrowded and which have cultural norms that are too ambivalent or weak to restrain people. Pathological incest occurs in families in which one or both of the parents is mentally ill or mentally retarded. Incest through object fixation refers to an incestuous act that is simply one manifestation of sexual fixation which puts all children in jeopardy. Psychopathic incest describes those normally functioning males who know that sexual behavior with children is wrong yet persist in the behavior despite that knowledge.

48. Brown, S. "Clinical Illustrations of the Sexual Misuse of Girls." **Child Welfare,** 58(7): 435-442, July/August 1979.

Sexual misuse refers to the exposure of a child to sexual stimulation inappropriate for the child's age, level of psychosexual development and role in the family. The dynamics of paternal incest as they are presented in the literature are reviewed.

49. Cohen, T. "The Incestuous Family." **Social Casework,** 62(8): 494-497, October 1981.

The dynamics of incest with special reference to the paternally incestuous family are reviewed.

50. Elwell, M.E. "Sexually Assaulted Children and Their Families." **Social Casework,** 60(4): 227-235, April 1979.

The literature is reviewed as to the rate, definition, effects, characteristics and nature of the incestuous relationship.

51. Forward, S. and Buck, C. **Betrayal of Innocence: Incest and Its Devastation.** Los Angeles, California: J.P. Tarcher, 1978.

Twenty-five cases of incest are used to illustrate the dynamics of incestuous families and the effects of incest on the victims.

52. Gentry, C.E. "Incestuous Abuse of Children: The Need for an Objective View." **Child Welfare,** 57(6): 355-364, June 1978.

The dynamics of paternal incest, the role the family members may play in it, and the effects that abuse may have on the victims are discussed. Treatment considerations are also presented.

53. Renshaw, D.C. and Renshaw, R.H. "Incest." **Journal of Sex Education and Therapy,** 3: 3-7, 1977.

Psychological, biological, sociological, moral and legal origins of the incest taboo are discussed. The effect that incest has on the family system and on the victim are presented.

54. Summit, R. and Kryso, J.A. "Sexual Abuse of Children: A Clinical Spectrum." **American Journal of Orthopsychiatry,** 48(2): 237-251, April 1978.

Several types of incest are proposed. Incidental incest involves the parent's attempt to cope indirectly with his erotic interest and dependency on children; ideological incest occurs when the parent attempts to rationalize his act by insisting that incest is good for the child. Psychotic incest is rare and involves the mentally ill parent turning the child into an object in his delusional system. Rustic environment incest occurs in areas of geographical and social isolation and may be more mythical than real. True endogamous incest occurs in severely dysfunctional families and misogynous incest symbolizes a hatred and fear of women in general. Pedophilic incest is an erotic interest in children in general and perverse incest occurs in loose sex cultures in which sexual experimentation occurs. A man who reigns as emperor in his own home may engage in imperious incest, rationalizing that his family must at all times be under his control. Finally, child rape is perpetrated by chronically antisocial individuals.

Incestuous Fathers

There are essentially three sources of data on the incestuous father. The first emerges from references on the nature of the paternally incestuous family nearly all of which, despite their varying theoretical orientations, describe to some extent the characteristics of fathers who sexually victimize their daughters.

The second source of data is found in original research which uses samples of incestuous fathers in order to draw conclusions. While this is certainly the most reliable and valid manner by which to collect data and make observations, it poses what may be a critical problem: most subjects for this research are drawn from prison or psychiatric hospital settings. If most cases of incest are never disclosed to reporting agencies, a fact that is frequently found in the literature, and if only a few of those cases that are reported result in the conviction or the commitment of the offender, then the subjects who comprise these samples in the original research may share characteristics that make them different from incestuous fathers in general. Perhaps that uniqueness lies in their psychological profile, or perhaps it is a product of the nature of their offense against their children, its frequency, or its duration; regardless, it may make them different in some qualitative way from other incestuous fathers.

The third source of data on incestuous fathers tends to counterbalance the bias found in the original research. This source is derived from studies of incest victims who are asked to describe their fathers and to make assessments of their general level of functioning. Since the vast majority of these fathers had never been incarcerated or committed as a result of their offenses, they may represent the "typical" incest offender.

Original Research

The following references in the literature represent original studies on the incestuous father. Care has been taken in each to describe the setting in which the research was conducted, the sample size, the operational definition of incest used, and the nature of the control group, if one was utilized in the design.

55. Berest, J.J. "Medico-Legal Aspects of Incest." **Journal of Sex Research,** 4(3): 195-205, August 1968.

One hundred incestuous fathers committed to the Lima State Hospital for treatment had engaged in sexual intercourse with their daughters. Most of the men are diagnosed as psychopathic or alcoholic or both, and all of them are judged as "psychiatrically abnormal."

56. Cavallin, H. "Incestuous Fathers: A Clinical Report." **American Journal of Psychiatry,** 122: 1132-1138, 1966.

Twelve incestuous fathers referred for treatment by the prison or the parole board were administered intelligence tests and the MMPI. All have average intelligence and no history of mental health problems, yet all engage in paranoic thinking in which the defense mechanism of projection is utilized. Their victimized daughters represent in their unconscious minds their own mothers who were absent or incapacitated during their childhood. Incest, then,

symbolically represents the desire for an incestuous relationship with their own mothers, or it represents an act of hostility against them for their emotional deprivation and abandonment.

57. Cormier, B.M.; Kennedy, M.; and Sangowicz, J.
"Psychodynamics of Father-Daughter Incest." **Canadian
Psychiatric Association Journal**, 7(5): 203-217, October
1962.
    Twenty-seven incestuous fathers who are either incar-
cerated or undergoing psychotherapy are of average intelligence, have sound employment histories, and except for
the incest, demonstrate no sexually perverse behavior. Each
tended to exploit his role in the family and that dynamic,
coupled with alcohol abuse, overcrowded living conditions,
and the absence or incapacitation of his wife, created conditions that precipitated the incest. The subjects initially
denied their involvement and when later acknowledging
it, tended to displace blame on their daughters. Two extensive
case studies illustrate these findings.

58. de Young, M. **The Sexual Victimization of Children.**
Jefferson, N.C.: McFarland, 1982.
    Fifty-five paternal incest offenders referred by court
and social service agencies tend to overcompensate for
their lack of parenting skills by assuming a patriarchal control
over their families. Using extensive rationalizations to disavow
their deviance, they tend to displace responsibility for their
behavior on their daughters. They are dependent, self-involved,
and tend to sexualize affection. Variations on this basic
profile are also presented.

59. Gebhard, P.H.; Gagnon, J.H.; Pomeroy, W.; and
Christenson, C. **Sex Offenders: An Analysis of Types.** New
York: Harper and Row, 1965.
    Incarcerated incest offenders are compared to other
types of incarcerated sex offenders and to a control group.
Incest offenders tend to assuage their guilt by developing
elaborate rationalizations that displace the responsibility
for the incest on the victim, the family, or on society. Compared to other offenders and the control group, they are
more intelligent, but they had engaged in the most sexual
activity and play as youngsters, were more likely to come
from deprived backgrounds, and had been raised in tense,
conflictual families. The majority are "endogamic," that

is, they are withdrawn, dependent persons who are unhealthily emotionally enmeshed with their families.

60. Julian, V. and Mohr, C. "Father-Daughter Incest: Profile of the Offender." **Victimology: An International Journal**, 4(4): 348-360, 1979.

Using the data base of the National Study on Child Neglect and Abuse Reporting Project, the authors examine 102 reported cases of paternal incest and compare them to a comparable number of cases of physical abuse reported to the project. The incestuous father has more children, a higher average annual income, and a lower rate of unemployment than the physically abusive father. Higher rates of alcoholism, mental health problems, and spouse abuse are also documented for incestuous fathers.

61. Justice, B. and Justice, R. **The Broken Taboo.** New York: Human Sciences Press, 1979.

Several types of incestuous fathers emerge from this study of 112 incestuous families. The "teacher" convinces himself that the incestuous act with his daughter is beneficial to her and prepares her for later sexual relationships. The "sexually liberated" father engages in incest as one manifestation of his generally sexually exploitative behavior. The "authoritarian" father exploits his role in the family and sees his children as possessions. The occasional incestuous father, finally, may consider himself to be "superior" to others; interested in preserving the bloodline, the goal of his sexual relationship with his daughter is to produce children.

62. Kirkland, K.D. and Bauer, C.A. "MMPI Traits of Incestuous Fathers." **Journal of Clinical Psychology,** 38(3): 645-649, July 1979.

It is hypothesized that a certain personality type may be common among incestuous fathers. The authors compare ten incestuous fathers with ten controls who had been matched for age, race and religion. The incestuous fathers are significantly more likely to have pathologically elevated scores on the MMPI in psychopathic deviation, psychasthenia, and schizophrenia, producing a profile of a chronically insecure, socially isolated person who has a marked tendency to act out. Described as passive-dependent, he has strong needs for affection and attention, and serious doubts about his masculinity. His judgment is poor and his ability to control his impulses is impaired; he lacks empathy in interpersonal relationships and has a tendency to manipulate others in order to get his own needs met.

63. Maisch, H. **Incest.** New York: Stein and Day, 1972.

The sample of seventy-eight court-referred incestuous fathers from West Germany frequently exploit their authoritative role within the family and occasionally use threats and violence to assert that patriarchal power.

64. Panton, J.H. "MMPI Profile Configurations Associated with Incestuous and Nonincestuous Child Molesting." **Psychological Reports,** 45(1): 335–338, 1979.

The MMPI profiles of thirty-five incarcerated incest offenders are compared to those of twenty-eight incarcerated nonincestuous child molesters. The incest offenders have a significantly higher elevated social introversion scale indicating that they are more inept in social skills and relationships and tend to be more shy, and less able to exercise competent decision making skills. Both groups had highly elevated psychopathic deviation scales, and significantly elevated depression, psychasthenia, and hysteria scales. These results suggest that both incest offenders and nonincestuous child molesters are nonaggressive, character-disordered individuals who experience a great deal of anxiety, feelings of inadequacy, and self-alientation.

65. Peters, J.J. "Children Who Are Victims of Sexual Assault and the Psychology of the Offender." **American Journal of Psychotherapy,** 30(3): 398–421, July 1976.

A battery of psychological tests was administered to a total of 224 probationed incest offenders, rapists, exhibitionists and homosexuals. The incest offenders have the lower average intelligence and the most somatic complaints as measured by the Cornell Medical Index. They perform better than the rapists but worse than the exhibitionists and the homosexuals on the Bender-Gestalt which measures ego integration. The Hand Test reveals that incest offenders are more assertive and less anxious than the homosexuals; the House-Tree-Person test results suggest they have less confusion about sexual roles than the rapist, but a higher level of anxiety regarding body structure and function. More submissive and suspicious than the rapists as measured by the Cattell Personality Inventory, the incest offenders nonetheless have a higher self-esteem as measured by the Self-Rating Scale. Finally, the Rorschach shows that the incest offenders are more passive than the rapists and have more insensitivity to the needs of others.

66. Quinsey, V.L.; Chaplin, T.C.; and Carrington, W.F.

"Sexual Preference Among Incestuous and Nonincestuous Child Molesters." **Behavior Therapy**, 10(4): 562-565, September 1979.

Nine convicted incest offenders are given a standard test of sexual preference in which penile circumference responses are measured while viewing slides of persons of varying ages and both sexes. The results are compared to those of seven convicted nonincestuous child molesters and suggest that the incest offenders have more appropriate age preferences, therefore the age of their daughters is not a factor that sufficiently explains the motivation to engage in an incestuous relationship.

67. Scheurell, R.P. and Rinder, I.P. "Social Networks and Deviance: A Study of Lower Class Incest, Wife-Beating and Non-Support Offenders." **Wisconsin Sociologist**, 10(2-3): 56-73, Spring 1973.

Ten incestuous fathers are compared to a comparable number of wife abusers and non-support offenders. Although all three groups have segregated patterns of role performance, the incest offenders show the greatest disparity between their behavior and the role expectations of the larger society, and are considerably more socially isolated.

68. Weiner, I.B. "Father-Daughter Incest: A Clinical Report." **Psychiatric Quarterly**, 36(4): 607-632, 1962.

Five court and self-referred incestuous fathers are administered a battery of psychological tests that include the WAIS, the Bender-Gestalt, the TAT, and the Rorschach. The test results reveal persons of average intelligence with well integrated defense systems. Paranoic trends in thinking are pronounced and problems over sexual identity are marked. There is a propensity to view people in segments or in caricatures and a tendency to devalue others as an expression of hostility. Incest may be an act through which the fathers, who had identified with their daughters, are able to achieve through fantasy the wished for gratification of their own fathers.

69. Weinberg, S.K. **Incest Behavior**. New York: Citadel, 1955.

Most incestuous fathers are "endogamic," that is, they have ingrown personalities and confine their sexual objects to family members because they are unwilling and unable to cultivate sexual contacts with persons outside of the family. Although dependent and shy, these fathers are also arrogant and domineering, especially within the family setting.

Descriptive Studies

Another source of information about incestuous fathers is derived from retrospective accounts of incest victims. Although lacking empirical validation, they nonetheless provide an interesting source of data as to how the victimized daughters perceive their fathers. Other types of descriptive studies include literature reviews and theoretical considerations, both of which advance the knowledge about the feelings, attitudes, motivations and behaviors of fathers who sexually victimize their daughters.

70. Conte, J.R. "Progress in Treating the Sexual Abuse of Children." **Social Work,** 29(3): 258-262, May/June 1984.

One core belief about incest is that the incestuous father is giving sexual expression to nonsexual needs and is therefore not inclined to sexually abuse children outside of his own family. Data from published studies are presented to challenge that belief that assumes that incest offenders and nonincestuous child molesters constitute two distinct clinical categories.

71. Frude, N. "The Sexual Nature of Sexual Abuse: A Review of the Literature." **Child Abuse and Neglect,** 6(2): 211-223, 1982.

Characteristics of incestuous fathers are reviewed in the literature and the theory is advanced that they often have unfulfilled sexual needs that because of a host of individual and family dynamics lead them to find their own children to be sexually attractive. This theory has often been underplayed or overlooked in the professional literature which has focused on power, control and violence, rather than sexual gratification, as the motivations for paternal incest.

72. Herman, J.L. **Father–Daughter Incest.** Cambridge, Massachusetts: Harvard University Press, 1981.

Forty victims of paternal incest retrospectively describe their fathers as patriarchs whose authority in the family was absolute and often asserted by force. Most were hard workers who were able to economically provide for their families, and some had achieved a significant amount of success for their endeavors. Their unfulfilled dependency needs were strong, and a great deal of retrospective evidence is provided that suggests that the fathers had experienced the sexual act with their daughters as powerfully reinforcing.

73. Meiselman, K.C. **Incest: A Psychological Study of Causes and Effects with Treatment Recommendations.** San Francisco: Jossey-Bass, 1978.

Accounts of fifty-eight victims of paternal incest are used to create the following classification of incestuous fathers. The endogamic father is heavily dependent on his family for the satisfaction of both his emotional and his sexual needs. The psychopathic incestuous father has little attachment to his daughter and his behavior is simply one manifestation of his generally exploitative behavior. The psychotic father has experienced severe ego disintegration; the drunken father has episodic periods of dyscontrol while under the influence of alcohol. Generally attracted sexually to children, the pedophilic incestuous father puts all children at risk for sexual abuse. Low intelligence is thought to reduce ego controls for the mentally defective father; and the situationally incestuous father only engages in incest during periods of overwhelming and unmanageable stress that interferes with his mature and healthy functioning.

74. Spencer, J. "Father-Daughter Incest: A Clinical View From the Corrections Field." **Child Welfare**, 57(9): 581-589, November 1978.

Observations of convicted incestuous fathers show that they tend to be paranoic in their thinking, with rigid defensive structures. Some are religious fanatics, some are alcoholic, and all demonstrate deep-seated insecurities about their own masculinity.

75. Swift, C. "The Prevention of Sexual Child Abuse: Focus on the Perpetrator." **Journal of Clinical Child Psychology**, 8(2): 133-136, Summer 1979.

The prevention of child sexual abuse begins with understanding two things about the offenders: they usually have experienced sexual abuse themselves as children, and they are sexually ignorant. Case studies and references from the literature support these two hypotheses. Prevention, then, must incorporate the prompt therapeutic intervention with sexually molested boys, and public education about sexuality in general and sexual abuse in particular.

Mothers of Incest Victims

The role of the mother in the paternally incestuous family is the subject of a great deal of speculation in the professional literature. Some researchers have targeted her for blame, assessing her role in the incest as primarily collusive in nature, and focusing on the secondary gains she experiences as a result of her daughter's victimization. In recent years, largely although not solely due to the introduction of the feminist perspective on incest, the mother is viewed as a victim of her husband's patriarchy, that same patriarchy that creates a family environment conducive to incest.

Two sources of data on the mother in paternally incestuous families are discovered in the literature. The first is found in original research on the role and the characteristics of the mother, and the second is derived from the retrospective descriptions of the mother by her incestuously victimized daughter.

Original Research

The literature contains some references which describe samples of mothers from paternally incestuous families. Although not subjected to the same sophisticated assessment as is utilized with incestuous fathers, these studies provide an objective analysis of the role of the nonparticipating mother in incest.

76. Browning, D.H. and Boatman, B. "Incest: Children at Risk." **American Journal of Psychiatry,** 134(1): 69-72, January 1977.

Fourteen incest victims referred to a child psychiatry clinic for treatment were accompanied by their mothers whose physical and/or emotional absence in the family afforded the opportunity for the incest to occur. All of the mothers are chronically depressed, and have subservient, subordinate relationships with their husbands.

77. de Young, M. **The Sexual Victimization of Children.** Jefferson, N.C.: McFarland, 1982.

Early childhoods characterized by emotional insecurity and physical and/or sexual abuse are documented in this sample of eight court-referred mothers of paternal incest victims. Eager to escape the tension of their own homes, the women married early and developed a passive, detached style of coping with their husbands' patriarchy and frequent physical abuse. Most of the mothers had sexually withdrawn from their husbands before the overt incest had occurred and had affected a role reversal with their daughters, encouraging them to assume a "little mother" role in the family. Once the overt incest began, the mothers frequently denied its occurrence and did not believe their daughters when the incest was finally disclosed.

78. Garrett, T.B. and Wright, R. "Wives of Rapists and Incest Offenders." **Journal of Sex Research,** 11(2): 149-157, May 1975.

Nine wives of incest offenders are compared to nine wives of forcible rapists. The wives of incest offenders are better educated and experience satisfaction from their husbands' deviance and subsequent incarceration. Although each expressed surprise that the incest had actually occurred, none of the wives contemplated divorce. Their husbands' deviance appears to be a useful lever used by the wives to build or reinforce a position of moral and social dominance within the family.

79. Justice, B. and Justice R. **The Broken Taboo.** New York: Human Sciences Press, 1979.

Nonparticipating mothers in 112 incestuous families have consistent qualities and styles of coping that include one or more of the following: a role reversal with the daughter; a sexual withdrawal from the husband; a submissive, weak style of interacting with the family; an indifference, absence, or incapacitation that creates emotional withdrawal from the family. Although most of the mothers denied that the incest was occurring, all were aware of it on some level and cognizant of the collusive role they played in it.

80. Kaufman, I.; Peck, A.L.; and Tagiuri, C.K. "The Family Constellation and Overt Incestuous Relations Between Father and Daughter." **American Journal of Orthopsychiatry,** 24(2): 266-277, 1954.

Mothers of eleven child incest victims referred for therapy use denial as a mechanism for coping with the incest. Often emotionally dependent, with feelings of worthlessness and helplessness, the mothers abdicate their maternal responsibility and create a role reversal with their daughters that sets the stage for the overt incest to begin. The mothers come from unhappy families in which they had experienced

a tense and unsatisfying relationship with their own mothers.
All had left home at a young age and had married early
to controlling and frequently physically violent men.

81. Kroth, J.A. **Child Sexual Abuse.** Springfield, Illinois:
Charles C. Thomas, Publisher, 1979.

A sample of 103 mothers of incest victims referred
for treatment at the Child Sexual Abuse Treatment Program
of Santa Clara County, California demonstrate that most
knew or at least suspected that the incest was occurring
but did not immediately take action to intercede on behalf
of their daughters. This high degree of collusion by the mothers and their unwillingness or inability to try and remedy
the situation is predictive of the degree of long-term deleterious consequences of the incest that their daughters are
likely to experience.

82. Lukianowicz, N. "Incest I: Paternal Incest; Incest
II: Other Types of Incest." **British Journal of Psychiatry,**
120(556): 301-313, March 1972.

Ten of the twenty-six mothers in this Northern Ireland
sample of paternal incest cases knew that the incest was
occurring but had adopted a "peace at any price" attitude
and did not intervene. All of the mothers appear to be hard-
working, intelligent, long-suffering women who are overwhelmed with child care responsibilities.

83. Lustig, N.; Dresser, J.W.; Spellman, S.W.; and Murray, T.B. "Incest: A Family Group Survival Pattern." **Archives
of General Psychiatry,** 14(1): 31-40, January 1966.

The six mothers of incest victims in this sample have
an early history of parental desertion and/or institutionaliza-
tion which created strong and unresolved dependency needs.
Marrying early, the women passively accepted their husbands'
authority and coped with their violence and threats by withdrawing emotionally and at times physically from their families. This withdrawal, in turn, thrusts the daughters into
a mothering role, setting the stage for the overt incest to
begin.

84. Maisch, H. **Incest.** New York: Stein and Day, 1972.

Some of the mothers in this sample of seventy-eight
court referred incest cases were seriously ill or otherwise
incapacitated at the time the incest was occurring. Some
had sexually withdrawn from their husbands prior to the
incest, and others had promiscuously sexually acted out

with men outside of the family. All had to some extent com-
promised their maternal role in the family and in doing so
rendered themselves incapable of protecting their daughters
from their husbands' sexual advances.

85. Weinberg, S.K. **Incest Behavior.** New York: Citadel,
1955.
Father-daughter incest is most likely to occur in families
in which the mothers do not assume a "restraining agent"
role. In this sample of 203 reported cases, the mothers tended
to relinquish their power in the family and failed to serve
both as a reality contact and a protector of their children.
Frequently masochistic, the wives are victimized by their
husbands and lack the assertiveness and necessary coping
skills to protect either themselves or their children.

Descriptive Studies

The retrospective accounts of victimized daughters
who describe their perception of their mothers' roles and
behaviors in the family have provided a wealth of data which
have not only contributed to the knowledge about the nonparticipating parent in the incestuous family, but which have
also increased understanding about the incestuous family
as a system. Some of the studies are more theoretical in
nature, reviewing and analyzing data from the literature
in order to create a richer portrait of the mothers in paternally incestuous families.

86. Brooks, B. "Preoedipal Issues in a Postincest Daughter." **American Journal of Psychotherapy,** 37(1): 129-136,
January 1983.
One case of a twenty-six year old incest victim is
presented to illustrate the theory that the preoedipal relationship between the child and the mother is an important compo-
nent in understanding incest, and may help to explain the
postincest self-destructive behavior of the victim. The literature is reviewed to support this theory.

87. Burgess, A.W.; Groth, A.N.; Holmstrom, L.L.; and
Sgroi, S.M. **Sexual Assault of Children and Adolescents.**
Lexington, Massachusetts: Lexington Books, 1978.
The mother's role in incest always involves some denial.
Having withdrawn from a sexual relationship with her husband,
she creates a role reversal with her daughter.

88. Dietz, C.A. and Craft, J.L. "Family Dynamics of Incest: A New Perspective." **Social Casework,** 61(10): 602-609, December 1980.

Protective Services workers from the Iowa Department of Social Services were surveyed as to their assessment of the role of the nonparticipating mother in paternally incestuous families. Based upon their experiences, most workers viewed the mothers as passive and submissive, as having been frequently abused by their husbands, and as being collusively involved in the incest.

89. Finkelhor, D. **Sexually Victimized Children.** New York: The Free Press, 1979.

A survey with questions about childhood sexual experiences with adults and children, incestuous sexual experiences, and coercive sexual experiences at any age was administered to 796 New England college and university students. Of the 530 female respondents, seven reported incestuous experiences with a natural father or a stepfather. Data from these respondents demonstrate that mothers are important in preventing child sexual abuse since they contribute significantly to either their daughters' resistance or vulnerability to sexual victimization. When mothers do not model self-protective behavior, do not provide their daughters with adequate sexual information, and do not supervise them, the likelihood of both incestuous and nonincestuous victimization of their daughters increases significantly.

90. Herman, J.L. **Father-Daughter Incest.** Cambridge, Massachusetts: Harvard University Press, 1981.

Forty adult women in psychotherapy for incest-related problems describe their mothers as playing an inferior role to their fathers in the family. Most were dependent economically and emotionally on their husbands and tolerated physical and verbal abuse in order to get these needs met. Encumbered with the care of many small children, they were described as having been in no position to challenge their husbands' domination, resist their abuse, or protect their children.

91. McIntyre, K. "Role of Mothers in Father-Daughter Incest: A Feminist Analysis." **Social Work,** 26(6): 462-466, November 1981.

The literature on incest has scapegoated the mothers in paternally incestuous families by accusing them of collusively setting up the incest; by overemphasizing the nonfulfillment of their roles as wives and mothers; by unfairly characterizing their personalities; and by critically assessing their reactions to the incest when it is disclosed. These techniques tend to shift the blame for the incest on the mothers, an example of "nonconscious ideology" in which sexism is subtly and covertly expressed, often in supposedly egalitarian terms. A feminist perspective on the mothers' roles views them as victims of their husbands' patriarchy and of the larger society's paternalism which teaches women to define themselves by the needs, desires and accomplishments of their husbands and to accept blame when these needs are not fulfilled.

92. Meiselman, K.C. **Incest: A Psychological Study of Causes and Effects with Treatment Recommendations.** San Francisco: Jossey-Bass, 1978.

Thirty mothers of incest victims were described by their daughters as having denied the incest because of their collusive roles in its initiation and continuation, or because of their unwillingness to face the difficulties they would experience if the incest were disclosed or terminated. The mothers are weak figures in the family, lacking in self-protective coping skills, and so emotionally and economically dependent on their husbands that they do not want to jeopardize their marriages by intervening in the incest.

Siblings of Incest Victims

Very few references in the literature have examined the role of siblings of incest victims in incestuous families, or the effects that vicarious participation can have on them.

93. Berry, G.W. "Incest: Some Clinical Variations on a Classical Theme." **Journal of the American Academy of Psychoanalysis,** 3: 151-161, 1975.

Daughters who are aware that their fathers are sexually victimizing their sisters may experience "incest envy." Jealous of what they perceive to be the special attention and affection given to the sisters by their fathers, these siblings may later experience overwhelming guilt feelings because of that envy and may experience psychological problems later in life. Two cases are presented to illustrate this theory.

94. de Young, M. "Siblings of Oedipus: Brothers and Sisters of Incest Victims." **Child Welfare,** 60(8): 561-568, September/October 1981.

Siblings of incest victims live within the same pathological family environment as the victim and are just as
likely to be negatively affected by the role reversals, power
shifts, blurred generational boundaries, and poor communication patterns as is the victim. Some siblings experience
envy if they are aware that the incest is occurring; others
are frightened that they will be victimized and will collusively
participate in setting up a sibling for victimization. Because
of these family dynamics and the coping styles adopted
by the siblings, antisocial and/or self-destructive behavior
may be noted for them as well as for the incest victim.

95. Heims, L.W. and Kaufman, I. "Variations on a Theme
of Incest." **American Journal of Orthopsychiatry**, 33(2):
311-312, 1963.
Some of the twenty disturbed adolescents who were
referred for treatment of incest-related problems report
being the "unchosen incest object" in that they had witnessed
incest occurring between their fathers and their siblings,
but were not directly victimized themselves. They described
feelings of rejection, envy, and a premature sexual stimulation, all of which contributed to behavioral and emotional
problems.

Role of the Child Victim

None of the cast of characters in paternally incestuous
families plays a more controversial role than the child victim.
Her behavior is viewed as existing on a continuum between
provocative seduction and innocent victimization.
The role that the child may play in the incest is more
than a rhetorical debate. The assessment of the child's responsibility for the incest also determines the extent to which
the researcher will consider the possible deleterious effects
of the victimization. Those researchers who place responsibility on the child for her own victimization, as an example,
are less inclined to consider the possibility that incest can
have harmful repercussions; after all, the likelihood of a
child being traumatized by an act that she wants and encourages is quite minimal. The counterargument offered in the
literature is that because of her age and level of social skills,
the child can be nothing more than an innocent victim, and
because of that innocence, incest is invariably experienced
as victimizing and traumatic.

Blame/Responsibility

The following references ascribe some degree of responsibility for the incest to the child victim. Some view the child as solely responsible, thereby effectively exonerating the father for his behavior; others assess a lesser degree of culpability, yet still perceive the child as playing an active role in the initiation and the continuation of the incest.

96. Howard, H.S. "Incest—The Revenge Motive." **Delaware State Medical Journal,** 31: 223–225, 1959.

Inferring that because the daughters are so often hostile to their fathers after the incest has terminated, they must have hostilely seduced their fathers in the first place. The daughters do not consciously accept responsibility for their behavior, but displace the blame on their fathers in an attempt to express hostile revenge against both of their parents and to elicit sympathy from others.

97. Henderson, D.J. "Incest: A Synthesis of Data." **Canadian Psychiatric Association Journal,** 17(4): 299–313, 1972.

A review of the literature supports the view that daughters collude in incestuous relationships with their fathers and will only disclose the incest to others in an attempt to get revenge when their fathers' interest in them begins to decrease.

98. Lukianowicz, N. "Incest I: Paternal Incest; Incest II: Other Types of Incest." **British Journal of Psychiatry,** 120(556): 301–313, March 1972.

The twenty-six incest victims in this Northern Ireland sample are described as being far from innocent victims; instead, they are viewed as willing partners and provocative seductresses. The passivity of the victims during the incest, their unwillingness to disclose the incest, and their postincest sexual acting out are factors which bolster this perception of the victims.

99. Yates, A. "Children Eroticized by Incest." **American Journal of Psychiatry,** 139(4): 402–405, April 1982.

The assumption that children are always the unwilling, passive victims of incest is challenged on the basis of the findings of the psychiatric evaluations of forty child incest victims. Most of these children had been eroticized by the incest and as a result are unable to distinguish between erotic and nonerotic relationships, are readily orgasmic, and easily aroused by a variety of different circumstances, and are able to maintain a high level of arousal without orgasm. That eroticization causes the children to seek to continue the incest and to refrain from disclosing it to others, therefore despite their tender age, these children cannot truly be considered innocent victims.

Innocent Victims

On the other end of the continuum of victim responsibility are those researchers who believe that the child is always the innocent victim of incest. Acknowledging that the child may behave in a provocative manner, that pseudoseductiveness is viewed as being a product of both the individual psychology of the child and the family dynamics that are impacting on her.

100. Browning, D.H. and Boatman, B. "Incest: Children at Risk." **American Journal of Psychiatry**, 134(1): 69-72, January 1977.
Many of the fourteen children referred for psychiatric treatment for incest related problems are defective children, suffering from a variety of diseases and disorders that may cause them to be viewed from a different perspective by family members. Others of those children are special in that they have already experienced unusual life circumstances such as abandonment. Their need for attention and affection may be stronger because of these circumstances and in the eyes of an impulse-ridden father, their specialness may be seen as invitation to engage in sexual behavior.

101. de Young, M. "Innocent Seducer or Innocently Seduced? The Role of the Child Incest Victim." **Journal of Clinical Child Psychology**, 11(1): 56-60, Spring, 1982.
The victims' passivity during the incest, their reticence to disclose the victimization, their preincest promiscuity, their frequently seductive behavior during therapy, and the incestuous fathers' tendency to displace responsibility on the children for the incest, have all been used in the literature to support the contention that children seduce, encourage and enjoy the incest. However, when the familial context of the incest is taken into consideration, these factors are put into a different perspective and the culpability of the child diminishes considerably. That familial context

shows that the origins of the "seductive" behavior of incest victims lie in their identification with the aggressor; their attempts to cope with separation anxiety; their attention and affection seeking behavior; the new identity they assume when their fathers displace the blame for the incest on them; and their simple inability to resist because of a lack of self-protecting people in their families whose behavior they can model.

102. de Young, M. "Counterphobic Behavior in Multiply Molested Children." **Child Welfare**, 63(4): 333-339, July/August 1984.

Four children who seemed to have encouraged their repeated sexual victimization are examined. Their "seductive" behavior is explained as being a symptom of counterphobia, the attempt to master the anxiety created by the initial sexual victimization by unconsciously and compulsively confronting the source of that anxiety by recreating victimizing situations.

103. Gruber, K.J. "The Child Victim's Role in Sexual Assault by Adults." **Child Welfare**, 40(5): 305-311, May 1981.

Children often cooperate with adults who sexually approach them and then do not disclose the sexual victimization to others. The reasons for doing so may arise out of their fears of displeasing an adult; the promise of favors and treats by the adult; their enjoyment of the attention and affection; and other situational pressures. When these are taken into consideration, the child's responsibility for the initiation and continuation of the sexual victimization significantly diminishes.

Disclosure of Incest

If the child's responsibility in the incest is questionable, then so is the veracity of the child's allegations of incest. The following references deal with the believability of the child's disclosure of incest, and address the controversial issue about whether children fantasize about incest and make false reports on the basis of these fantasies.

104. Ferenczi, S. "Confusion of Tongues Between Adults and the Child." **International Journal of Psychoanalysis,** 30: 225-230, 1949.

Because of the overwhelming feelings of helplessness

and anxiety, very young children who have been victimized by an adult will experience confusion about whether the event actually occurred and may deny the reality of it when confronted by an adult.

105. Freud, S. "The Aetiology of Hysteria." **The Complete Psychological Works of Sigmund Freud,** translated by J. Strachey, Standard Edition. London, England: Hogarth Press, 1962.
Women suffering from hysteria often report experiences of childhood sexual abuse, frequently with a family member. These reports are to be treated skeptically since they may represent "defensive fiction," fantasies created by the patients on the basis of their own unacceptable incestuous wishes.

106. Kaplan, S.L. and Kaplan, S.J. "The Child's Accusation of Sexual Abuse During a Divorce and Custody Struggle." **Hillside Journal of Clinical Psychiatry,** 3(1): 81-95, 1981.
Divorce and custody hearings bring out extremes in behavior. A case of two siblings who accused their father of incest during a custody battle are presented and the dilemmas that their accusation created are discussed in detail. Although it is unclear as to whether one of the siblings had actually been incestuously abused, the allegation of the second sibling who had not really been abused is explained in terms of folie à deux, the transference of delusional material and/or abnormal behavior from one person to another who is in close association with the person primarily affected.

107. Masson, J.M. **The Assault on Truth: Freud's Suppression of the Seduction Theory.** New York: Farrar, Straus and Giroux, 1984.
Personal correspondence between Sigmund Freud and Wilhelm Fliess reveal that Freud initially believed that paternal incest as well as other types of child sexual abuse were the root cause of hysteria but that he revised that theory and relegated the allegations of sexual abuse to the fantasies of his patients because of his own difficulty in accepting the possibility that incest was so prevalent and because of his uncomfortable awareness of his own incestuous wishes toward his daughter.

108. Peters, J.J. "Children Who Are Victims of Sexual Assault and the Psychology of the Offender." **American Journal of Psychotherapy,** 30(3): 398-421, July 1976.

Seven cases of children who have made allegations of sexual abuse that were proven are presented and the cultural and personal factors that cause professionals to deny the reality of these disclosures are discussed in detail. Relegating these trauma to the imagination of children tends to divert treatment from dealing with the source of the problem, and although it may be a convenient assumption for the therapist, it is counterproductive for the most efficient resolution of the symptoms.

109. Rosenfeld, A.A.; Nadelson, C.C.; and Krieger, M. "Incest and Sexual Abuse of Children." **Journal of the American Academy of Child Psychiatry,** 16: 327-339, 1977.
When an actual traumatic incest event has occurred in childhood, it may be repressed, displaced, or substituted for a memory of a less traumatic event. Consequently, the child's disclosure of the incest may be vague, inconsistent, or casually delivered.

110. Rosenfeld, A.A.; Nadelson, C.C.; Krieger, M. "Fantasy and Reality in Patient Reports of Incest." **Journal of Clinical Psychiatry,** 40(4): 159-164, April 1979.
The line of demarcation between fantasy and reality is often hazy since the fantasy may be based upon real-life family experiences that have been displaced or distorted. Children over the age of nine who give a clear report of sexual victimization should be believed since it is at that age that a child is able to clearly differentiate between fantasy and reality; before that age, in the absence of corroborating evidence, reports should be treated skeptically. Therapists dealing with clients of any age who report sexual abuse should consider whether the disclosure could be an incorrectly reported fantasy from childhood; whether the family of the person was overstimulating; whether actual molestation has occurred but the wrong person is being accused; whether the person making the report is psychiatrically disturbed; whether there is an ulterior motive for making a false allegation; and whether there are extenuating circumstances such as a divorce or custody battle that may motivate the leveling of false charges.

111. Rush, F. "Freud and the Sexual Abuse of Children." **Chrysalis,** 1: 31-45, 1977.
The author discusses the reasons behind Freud's suppression of the seduction theory and his contention that children fantasize and incorrectly report allegations of incest.

4
Effects of Paternal Incest
on the Victims

It is generally agreed upon in the literature that incest is a harmful act that often has deleterious effects on the children. The nature and the severity of those effects are dependent on a number of different factors: the type of sexual abuse experienced, its frequency and duration, the integrity of the family system in which it occurs, and the preincest personality of the victim.

For the purpose of clarity, the references on the effects of incest are classified according to developmental stages of the victims under consideration and subcategorized, wherever possible, according to the major symptoms presented. Once again, the definitions of incest used in the various studies are important since they define the variable of the type of sexual abuse experienced; data as to frequency, duration, family system integrity, and preincest personality will also be noted if provided in the references.

Effects on Children

Less able to verbally share their anxieties and fears with adults and, in some cases, less likely to be believed when they do, children victimized by incest manifest a wide range of behavioral, emotional and somatic symptoms. The following references present the effects of incest on prepubertal children. Some of these references include adolescents in their samples, but in each presented in this section, the average age of the subjects is twelve or below. Two of the following studies also deal with children born of incestuous relationships.

112. Adams, M.S. and Neel, J.V. "Children of Incest." **Pediatrics,** 40: 55-62, 1967.

Eighteen children born of nuclear family incest are compared to a control group of children matched for age, race, weight, height, I.Q., and socioeconomic status. Both groups were examined at birth and again at six months. Seven of the eighteen children born of incest were normal and ready for adoption at six months; five had died in early infancy, two were severely retarded with seizures, three had borderline I.Q.'s, and one had a bilateral cleft palate. Fifteen of the eighteen children in the control group were normal and ready for adoption at six months.

113. Adams-Tucker, C. "Proximate Effects of Sexual Abuse in Childhood: A Report on Twenty-eight Children." **American Journal of Psychiatry,** 139(10): 1252-1256, October 1982.

The Louisville Behavior Checklist was administered to significant adults in the lives of twenty-eight sexually abused children. Most of the children, who ranged in age between $2\frac{1}{2}$ and $15\frac{1}{2}$, had been molested by their fathers. Test results indicate that the children are all symptomatic in one or more of the following areas: self-destructive, suicidal and/or withdrawing behavior; sexual complaints, running away and/or aggressive behavior; school, peer and/or parent problems; and anxiety, psychosomatic and/or sleep-related problems. The emotional disturbance suffered by the victims is most severe when the sexual abuse begins at an early age and continues repetitively over a long period of time; or when it begins in the adolescent years, even though its frequency and duration may be limited. All of the subjects experienced emotional and behavioral problems as serious as those of children seeking psychiatric help for any reason.

114. Brant, R.S.T. and Tisza, V.B. "The Sexually Misused Child." **American Journal of Orthopsychiatry,** 47(1): 80-90, January 1977.

Using a definition of sexual misuse as the exposure of a child to sexual stimulation inappropriate for the child's age, level of psychosexual development, and role in the family, this retrospective study of hospital emergency room logs discovered fifty-two cases of child sexual misuse treated in a year's period of time. The sexual misuse of infants usually produces reddened genitals, eating and sleeping disorders, and altered activity levels. Because toddlers and young children have difficulty in verbally expressing their anxiety, physical and behavioral symptoms may be present. Those include: genital irritation, discharge or infection; psychosomatic complaints, especially of stomach aches and dysuria; venereal disease; and a wide range of behavioral problems that includes enuresis, encopresis, hyperactivity, altered sleeping and eating patterns, phobias, compulsive behaviors, precocious sex play, excessive sexual curiosity, compulsive masturbation, deficits in attention, and separation anxiety.

115. Browning, D.H. and Boatman, B. "Incest: Children at Risk." **American Journal of Psychiatry,** 134(1): 69-72, January 1977.

Fourteen incestuously abused children between the ages of four and fifteen years present symptoms of psychosomatic complaints, anxiety, fearfulness, and acting out behaviors that include running away and sexual promiscuity.

116. de Young, M. "Innocent Seducer or Innocently Seduced? The Role of the Child Incest Victim." **Journal of Clinical Child Psychology,** 11(1): 56-60, Spring 1982.

Incestuously victimized children frequently behave in a pseudoseductive and pseudomature fashion. It is theorized that this behavior originates in the family due to the victim's identification with the aggressor; her attempt to cope with separation anxiety; her attention and affection seeking behavior; her new identity created by the displacement of blame onto her; and her simple inability to model self-protective behavior.

117. de Young, M. "Counterphobic Behavior in Multiply Molested Children." **Child Welfare,** 63(4): 333-339, July/August 1984.

Four young children who behaved seductively and seemed to have encouraged their repeated sexual victimization are examined. Their "seductive behavior" is viewed as a symptom of counterphobia, the attempt to master the anxiety created by the first sexual assault on them by unconsciously and compulsively confronting the source of that anxiety by creating victimizing situations.

118. Emslie, G.J. and Rosenfeld, A.A. "Incest Reported by Children and Adolescents Hospitalized for Severe Psychiatric Problems." **American Journal of Psychiatry,** 140(6): 708-711, June 1983.

Sixty-five children and adolescents hospitalized for severe psychiatric problems are surveyed as to a history of incest victimization. Of the nonpsychotic girls, 37% were incestuously victimized; 10% of the girls diagnosed as psychotic experienced incest; and 8% of all of the boys in the sample are incest victims. The single factor common to children and adolescents who suffer from serious psychopathology that requires psychiatric hospitalization is severe family disorganization and the ego impairment it creates, whether or not it is accompanied by incest.

119. Geiser, R.L. "Incest and Psychological Violence." **International Journal of Family Psychiatry,** 2(3-4): 291-300, 1981.

The adult's power, strength and authority lead the child to experience incest as an act of violence. Eating and sleeping disorders, somatic complaints, anxiety, hyperactivity, learning problems, sexual preoccupation and sexual acting out are all symptoms commonly seen in incestuously abused children. A review of the literature on incest suggests that less than one-quarter of all female victims emerge from their experiences without serious side effects, and that for most, the emotional effects are longterm and will persist into adulthood.

120. Gentry, C.E. "Incestuous Abuse of Children: The Need for an Objective View." **Child Welfare,** 57(6): 355-364, June 1978.

The young incest victim may find the sexual experience fascinating and pleasurable, but those initial reactions soon give way to feelings of uneasiness and even panic. Fearfulness is especially common, with fears of dying, of being rejected, and of being caught and punished frequently reported. Because the family may not support the victim when the incest is finally discovered, the child may change or recant his or her account of the victimization.

121. Johnson, M.S. "Recognizing the Incestuous Family." **Journal of the National Medical Association,** 75(8): 757-761, 1983.

Family physicians are encouraged to look for the following medical signs of incest in their young patients: vaginal discharge, abdominal pain, seizure disorder, enuresis or encopresis, venereal disease, pregnancy, urinary tract symptoms, headache, conversion symptoms, vaginsmus, insomnia, anorexia, and suicide attempts. Behavioral problems such as depression, poor grades in school, running away, drug abuse, promiscuity, and multiple somatization may also be evident, and physicians are urged to consider these problems within the context of the family by conducting a thorough family study of the patient.

122. Peters, J.J. "Children Who are Victims of Sexual Assault and the Psychology of the Offender." **American Journal of Psychotherapy,** 30(3): 398-421, July 1976.

Sixty-four victims of child sexual abuse between the ages of two and twelve show the following symptoms while being treated at a rape counseling center: fears of men, sleep problems, nightmares, anorexia, and school phobia. The most acute emotional problems are predicted for those children who were incestuously victimized by their fathers because they experience considerably more confusion and bewilderment within the family. Therapists are urged not to overlook the quiet, nonsymptomatic child, however, because that child may be less able to openly express his or her feelings and may have retreated into a protective state of emotional withdrawal.

123. Rosenfeld, A.A. "The Clinical Management of Incest and Sexual Abuse of Children." **Journal of the American Medical Association,** 242(6): 1761-1764, October 1977.

Clues to incest in young children are: genital complaints, venereal disease, compulsive masturbation, sexual acting out, and any unpredictable and extreme alterations in behavior.

124. Ruch, L.O. and Chandler, S.M. "The Crisis Impact of Sexual Assault on Three Victim Groups: Adult Rape Victims, Child Rape Victims, and Incest Victims." **Journal of Social Service Research,** 5(1-2): 83-100, 1982.

The impact of sexual assault as measured by a standardized assessment scale is determined for a group of 283 adult rape victims, 78 child rape victims, and 47 child incest victims. Data reveal that child incest victims experience significantly more emotional trauma than child rape victims, and that is probably due to the child's relationship with the offender and the fear of the consequences of the disclosure. Any victim's trauma level will be significantly higher if verbal threats, physical force, the use of a weapon, victim resistance, or injury to the victims are features of the sexual assault.

125. Sarles, R.M. "Incest." **Pediatric Clinics of North America,** 22(3): 633-642, August 1975.

Two cases of incestuously abused children who presented

somatic complaints of vaginal discharge, pelvic pain and hyperventilation are presented.

126. Schultz, L.G. and Jones, P. "Sexual Abuse of Children: Issues for Social Service and Health Professionals." **Child Welfare,** 62(2): 99–108, March/April 1983.

Indicators of incestuous abuse in young children include: nightmares, running away, poor peer relations, disruptive or aggressive behaviors, sexual self-consciousness, arriving early for school and leaving late, allegations of sexual mistreatment by siblings, and role reversal with the mother.

127. Seemanova, E. "A Study of Children of Incestuous Matings." **Human Heredity,** 21: 108–128, 1971.

A sample of 161 children born of incest was compared to a control group of 95 children who are half-siblings of the children born of incest. Retardation, congenital malformation, and multiple malformations are much more likely to be seen in children born of incest.

128. Sgroi, S.M. "Kids with Clap: Gonorrhea as an Indicator of Child Sexual Assault." **Victimology: An International Journal,** 2(2): 251–267, Summer 1977.

Gonorrhea infections in children in any body site except for the eyes is a tell-tale indicator of child sexual abuse. The examination of children in cases where sexual abuse is suspected should include a complete physical and developmental exam; skeletal x-rays for children under six years old; a genital exam with a vaginal smear; cultures of the throat, urethra, rectum and vagina as well as blood tests to screen for venereal disease.

129. Summit, R.C. "The Child Sexual Abuse Accommodation Syndrome." **Child Abuse and Neglect,** 7(2): 177–193, 1983.

The child abuse accommodation syndrome classifies the most typical reactions of a child to sexual abuse by describing the basic childhood vulnerabilities of accommodation and helplessness, and the child's reactions of secrecy, delayed and unconvincing disclosure, and retraction which are sequentially contingent upon sexual abuse.

130. Thomas, J.N. "Yes, You Can Help a Sexually Abused Child." **RN,** 43(8): 23–29, August 1980.

On the basis of the medical examinations of 500 sexually abused children, 200 of whom are incest victims, the following symptoms are most commonly noted: venereal disease; vaginal and/or rectal pain, swelling or bleeding; behavioral disturbances such as phobias, sudden irritability, regressive behavior, and decline in the quality of school performance; and behavioral problems such as running away, drug abuse, excessive masturbation, and sexually precocious behavior and comments.

131. Yates, A. "Children Eroticized by Incest." **American Journal of Psychiatry,** 139(4): 482-485, April 1982.

Psychiatric evaluations on forty young victims of incest show that children can become eroticized by incest and as a result are unable to distinguish between erotic and nonerotic relationships, are readily orgasmic and easily aroused by a variety of different circumstances, and are able to maintain a high level of arousal without orgasm. That eroticization causes the children to seek to continue the incest and to refrain from disclosing it to others. In addition, these children tend to be more anxious, depressed, underachieving, and demonstrate more somatic complaints and self-defeating behaviors than other children. Incest, however, may not be the sole cause of these emotional problems since physical abuse and neglect are frequently also features of incestuous families.

Effects on Adolescents

Symptoms of incestuous abuse tend to become more crystallized during adolescence. Now with a larger repertoire of coping skills, a more complex network of social interactions, and greater freedom and mobility, the adolescent's reactions to paternal incest are more likely to be played out in the public arena. Studies which focus on the effects of incest on the adolescent tend to describe symptoms in one of three clusters: compulsive and/or self-defeating acting out; emotional and/or psychological problems; and psychosomatic complaints.

Acting Out

The developmental stage of adolescence is normally characterized by rebellion, behavioral extremes and rule challenging behavior, but the incestuously victimized adolescent's acting out tends to assume a compulsive and self-defeating character that is in intensity and frequency qualitatively different than the acting out of nonvictimized adolescents. The following references examine what is generically referred to as acting out behavior.

132. Bigras, J. "On Disappointment and the Consequences of Incest in the Adolescent Girl." **Canadian Psychiatric Association Journal,** 11: 189-204, 1966.

Nine adolescent girls in a psychiatric facility for problems related to their having been sexually approached by a blood relative, are compared to three hospitalized girls who do not have a history of incest victimization. A "compulsive masochistic reaction" is documented for most of the incest victims who display self-destructive sexual acting out, running away, and suicide attempts.

133. de Young, M. **The Sexual Victimization of Children.** Jefferson, N.C.: McFarland, 1982.

Twelve adolescent paternal incest victims from a total sample of sixty victims show suicidal ideation or attempts, self-injuring behaviors, sexual acting out, psychosomatic complaints, psychological disturbance, and increased vulnerability to multiple sexual assaults. It is theorized that incest victimization seriously assaults the integrity of the ego so that self-esteem and self-protective coping skills are significantly impaired in victimized adolescents.

134. Gordon. L. "Incest as Revenge Against the Preoedipal Mother." **Psychoanalytic Review,** 42: 284-292, 1955.

Postincest sexual acting out by the adolescent victim is usually motivated by hostility towards the parents.

135. James, J. and Meyerding, J. "Early Sexual Experiences and Prostitution." **American Journal of Psychiatry,** 134(12): 1381-1385, December 1977.

In a study of twenty adolescent female prostitutes, thirteen experienced incestuous abuse in the home before turning to prostitution. A lack of parental guidance, the discovery that sex can be used to gain social status, the emotionally disruptive impact of incest, and an early negative labeling process are all thought to be experiences conducive to prostitution for adolescents.

136. James, K.L. "Incest: The Teenager's Perspective." **Psychotherapy: Theory, Research and Practice,** 14(2): 146-155, Summer 1977.

Of the eighty-five adolescent girls in a juvenile correctional facility in Washington state, 12% are incest victims. All demonstrate low self-esteem and a tendency to make self-depracatory remarks, a mistrust of men, running away behavior, and sexually provocative behavior.

137. Justice, B. and Justice, R. **The Broken Taboo.** New York: Human Sciences Press, 1979.

A pervasive damage to self-esteem, feelings of hopelessness, worthlessness and depression may be hallmarks of the adolescent incest victim. Acting out behavior may be aggressive, sexual or self-destructive in nature.

138. Kaufman, I.; Peck, A.L.; and Tagiuiri, C.K. "The Family Constellation and Overt Incestuous Behavior Between Father and Daughter." **American Journal of Orthopsychiatry,** 24(2): 266-277, 1954.

Eleven adolescent female incest victims referred for therapy experience considerable anxiety due to feelings of having been abandoned by their mothers. Sexual acting out, running away, somatic complaints and learning problems are also noted. The results of a battery of psychological tests including the Rorschach, TAT, Draw-A-Man, and intelligence tests reveal anxiety, depression, confusion over sexual identity, a fear of sex, and oral deprivation and oral sadism. Much of the acting out behavior is motivated by a need to be punished.

139. Knittle, B.J. and Tuana, S.J. "Group Therapy as Primary Treatment for Adolescent Victims of Intrafamilial Sexual Abuse." **Clinical Social Work Journal,** 8(4): 236-242, Winter 1980.

Incest victimization creates isolation, alienation, feelings of helplessness, distrust, guilt, shame and self-defeating and self-destructive behaviors. A group therapy model is particularly helpful in resolving these problems for adolescent victims of incest.

140. Maisch, H. **Incest.** New York: Stein and Day, 1972.

In a sample of seventy-eight court referred cases, the victims demonstrate a tendency to act out sexually and antisocially with behaviors such as lying and stealing. Hypothesizing that these behaviors developed before the overt incest took place, they are viewed as parts of a larger pattern of character disorder that develops within members of pathological families.

141. Medlicott, R.W. "Parent-Child Incest." **Australia and New Zealand Journal of Psychiatry,** 1: 180-187, 1967.

Seventeen adolescent victims of incest, identified through social service agencies and residential treatment centers for delinquent girls, have a documented history of sexually promiscuous behavior, antisocial acting out, and lesbianism.

142. Meiselman, K.C. **Incest: A Psychological Study of Causes and Effects with Treatment Recommendations.** San Francisco: Jossey-Bass, 1978.

Eleven adolescent victims of paternal incest demonstrate pseudomaturity, sexually inappropriate behavior with peers and children, and emotional disturbance.

143. Reich, J.W. and Guitierres, S.E. "Escape/Aggression Incidence in Sexually Abused Juvenile Delinquents." **Criminal Justice and Behavior,** 6(3): 239-243, September 1979.

The data in this study of 747 juvenile offenders who committed "escape" crimes such as running away and truancy, and "aggressive" crimes such as assault and armed robbery, reveal that 55% of the escape crimes were committed by incestuously abused adolescents. Only 5% of the aggressive crimes were committed by incest victims.

144. Simpson, C.A. and Porter, G.L. "Self-Mutilation in Children and Adolescents." **Bulletin of the Menninger Clinic,** 45(5): 428-438, July 1981.

This study of twenty adolescent self-mutilators examines the roles that physical abuse, a sense of abandonment in childhood, and incest play in self-injuring behavior. Thirteen of the adolescents in the sample were physically abused; twelve had experienced the death of a parent or abandonment by a parent; and nine were incestuously abused. All of the adolescents had experienced unusual disruptions in the early attachment process and as a result are unable to form stable, separate, independent personalities during adolescence. It is estimated that the rate of incest in the backgrounds of this sample of young self-mutilators may be significantly higher than what is reported in this study since adolescents are often reticent to disclose a history of incest victimization and family members are often resistant to verifying it.

145. Sloane, P. and Karpinski, E. "Effects of Incest on the Participants." **American Journal of Orthopsychiatry,** 12(4): 666-673, October 1942.

Each of the five adolescent incest victims in this study reacted to the abuse in her own way, depending on the predisposition of her personality, and on her ego and superego strengths. All of the victims in this sample tend to be compulsive, histrionic, and sexually promiscuous. Incest initiated in adolescence tends to have more deleterious effects than when it is initiated in childhood because of the increased strength of inhibiting factors in the postpubertal years.

Psychological Problems

Adolescent incest victims often experience psychological problems of varying severity. The following studies make specific reference to these symptoms and to the diagnosable mental illnesses that may be produced by the interference of incest with the predictable emotional development of young people.

146. de Young, M. **The Sexual Victimization of Children.** Jefferson, N.C.: McFarland, 1982.

Twelve adolescent victims of incest demonstrate a whole range of neurotic, psychosomatic, and behavioral symptoms that include depression, anxiety, sexual identity confusion, and intense feelings of helplessness, worthlessness and hopelessness.

147. Husain, A. and Chapel, J.L. "History of Incest in Girls Admitted to a Psychiatric Hospital." **American Journal of Psychiatry,** 140(5): 591-593, May 1983.

Defining incest as overt sexual intercourse occurring between members of a group who are not permitted by society to marry, a sample of 437 adolescent girls hospitalized in a psychiatric facility was surveyed as to their incestuous experiences. Sixty-one of the girls report incest; fifty-one of those had been victimized by their natural father or stepfather. All cases are verified by a review of the hospital and other social service agency records.

148. Maisch, H. **Incest.** New York: Stein and Day, 1972.

Psychological problems in adolescent incest victims range from character disorders, to neuroses, to psychosis. It is hypothesized on the basis of accounts of the girls' preincest personality that the incest caused personality disturbance in 35% of the cases, exacerbated existing symptoms in 27%, and had no traceable relation to personality problems in the remaining 38% of the girls.

149. Meiselman, K.C. **Incest: A Psychological Study of Causes and Effects with Treatment Recommendations.** San Francisco: Jossey-Bass, 1978.

Of the eleven victims who were interviewed during the incest affair or within a year of its termination, three are psychotic, two are severely neurotic, and three present mixed pictures of depression, anxiety and antisocial behavior. In approximately 50% of the sample, the symptoms presented are thought to have developed before the incest was initiated, although the stress produced by the incest is likely to have exacerbated them.

150. Molnar, G. and Cameron, P. "Incest Syndromes: Observations in a General Hospital Psychiatric Unit." **Canadian Psychiatric Association Journal,** 20: 1-24, 1975.

Ten adolescent girls, inpatients in a psychiatric hospital, have histories of incest victimization. All are experiencing depression, suicidal ideation, thoughts about running away, and sexual identity confusion. This cluster of symptoms may represent an "incest syndrome" and it is estimated that 5% of all commitments of adolescent girls involves this syndrome.

151. Saffer, J.B.; Sansone, P.; and Gentry, J. "The Awesome Burden Upon the Child Who Must Keep a Family Secret." **Child Psychiatry and Human Development,** 10(1): 35-40, Fall 1979.

Two cases of adolescents who were forced by their incestuous fathers to keep the incest secret and who developed psychotic symptoms because of this pressure, are described in detail.

Psychosomatic Complaints

The anxiety, rage and fear that so often accompany incest victimization may be directed toward the self. In those cases, a variety of psychosomatic behaviors may be noted, as are documented in the following references.

152. Goodwin, J.; Simms, M.; and Bergman, R. "Hysterical Seizures: A Sequel to Incest." **American Journal of Orthopsychiatry,** 49(4): 698-703, October 1979.

Six cases of hysterical seizures in adolescent incest victims are described. Additional problems with promiscuity, sexual dysfunction, running away from home, and suicidal ideation are presented by the girls. It is hypothesized that hysterical seizures may be a natural symptom choice because they replicate movements related to sexual stimulation as well as those related to the resistance of sexual assault. The sense of power reported by the girls during the seizures suggests that they are unconsciously exerting control over their own emotional tension as well as control over significant others. The seizures also serve to strengthen the defenses of denial, dissociation, and repression which are needed to forget the incest; also, by having the attacks in public, the girls can release tensions associated with keeping the incest a secret.

153. Gross, M. "Incestuous Rape: A Case for Hysterical Seizures." **American Journal of Orthopsychiatry,** 49(4): 704-708, October 1979.
Four adolescent girls who were incestuously raped have hysterical seizures that create significant secondary gains.

154. Gross, M. "Incest and Hysterical Seizures." **Medical Hypoanalysis,** 3(4): 146-152, November 1982.
Six cases of hysterical seizures in adolescent incest victims are described in detail. The similarity of the seizure to the sexual act is hypothesized as the unconscious motivation behind the choice of this symptom. The seizures become a way for the nonconscious mind to act out and abreact the incest trauma, relieving the ego of the tension associated with it.

155. LaBarbera, J.D. and Emmett, D. "Hysterical Seizures: The Role of Sexual Exploitation." **Psychosomatics,** 21(11): 897-903, December 1980.
Four cases of hysterical seizures, one of which was precipitated by incest, are described. Hysterical seizures can be prompted by sexually charged events for girls who exhibit ambivalence about sexual issues and sexual identity.

Effects on Adults

The sequelae of incest would suggest that some incest-related problems persist into adulthood. These longterm

effects may be placed in symptom clusters related to compulsive and/or self-defeating acting out; emotional and/or diagnosable psychological problems; and psychosomatic complaints.
During the adult years, however, when marriage, childrearing
and employment may take place, relationships problems
are more likely to emerge and this will constitute the fourth
category of the longterm effects of paternal incest on adults.
Finally, sexual problems are frequently reported by adult
survivors of incest and will be considered as a fifth category.

Most of the studies on incest have made reference
to the longterm effects it is likely to have on the adult;
in some of those studies, the comments or the speculations
about effects are little more than passing references or
short summations. The studies in this section focus largely
or exclusively on those longterm effects of paternal incest
on adult survivors.

Acting Out

As with the adolescent, many incest-related problems
are played out in the public arena by adult survivors and
take the form of deviant or antisocial behavior. The rage
and defiance that so often accompany these acts also may
be turned inward, producing self-defeating or self-injuring
behavior, or an increased vulnerability for further victimization, as the following references describe.

156. Brooks, B. "Preoedipal Issues in a Postincest Daughter." **American Journal of Psychotherapy,** 37(1): 129-136,
January 1983.

One case of a twenty-six year old incest victim is
presented to illustrate the theory that the preoedipal relationship between the child and the mother is an important compo-
nent to understanding incest, and may help to explain the
postincest self-destructive behavior of the victim. The literature is reviewed to support this theory.

157. Carroll, J.; Schaffer, C.; Spensley, J.; and Abramo-
witz, S.I. "Family Experiences of Self-Mutilating Patients."
American Journal of Psychiatry, 137(7): 852-853, July 1980.

Fourteen psychiatrically hospitalized self-mutilators
are compared to an equal number of hospitalized non-muti-
lating patients. Incest victimization in childhood or adolescence tends to have occurred significantly more often in
the histories of the self-mutilators. Incest, separation anxiety

and the threat of abandonment, disharmony in the parent-child relationship, and family violence are background factors that precipitate self-mutilating behavior.

158. de Young, M. "Self-Injurious Behavior in Incest Victims: A Research Note." **Child Welfare,** 61(8): 577-584, November/December 1981.

Twenty-six paternal incest victims in a sample of forty-five describe self-mutilating behavior during their adolescence and/or adulthood. That behavior is theorized to be a product of primitive, magical thinking in which the victim attempts to stop the incest by making herself unattractive, or tries to make herself look different so that people will inquire as to the motivation behind the self-injury. It is also a symptom of the introjection of the parents' hostility and abuse, and the victim's need to punish herself for what she may perceive to have been her collusive role in the incest. Finally, self-injurious behavior may be triggered by feelings of guilt, anger, fear and betrayal which overwhelm the ego's defenses; in those cases, the self-injuring act restores the ego's integrity and produces reintegration.

159. de Young, M. "Case Reports: The Sexual Exploitation of Incest Victims by Helping Professionals." **Victimology: An International Journal,** 6(1-4): 92-100, 1981.

Three cases of adult women who were sexually exploited by their therapists after disclosing a history of incest.

160. Green, C.M. "Filicidal Impulses as an Anniversary Reaction to Childhood Incest." **American Journal of Psychotherapy,** 36(2): 264-271, April 1982.

A thirty-four year old psychotherapy patient was successfully treated for filicidal impulses directed towards her five year old daughter whom she had attempted to strangle. These impulses developed out of an "anniversary reaction" in which the patient, who had been incestuously abused by her father beginning at the age of five, had projected her own childhood sexuality on her daughter, and in attempting to kill her was symbolically trying to destroy the part of herself that was consumed by intolerable sexual guilt. Filicide, in this case, is viewed as a form of extended suicide deriving from the woman's identification with her daughter.

161. Grunenbaum, H.V. and Klerman, G.L. "Wrist Slashing." **American Journal of Psychiatry,** 124(4): 527-534, October 1967.

Adult female psychiatric patients with a history of wrist-slashing behavior are found to be intelligent, talented and socially adept, but with intense feelings of being unloved and unwanted. The most striking feature of their early child-hoods is premature sexual experiences, most often incestuous in nature. It is hypothesized that family experiences of rejec-tion, open aggression, and incest lead to the development of ego deficits which under stress precipitate wrist-slashing behavior.

162. Malmquist, C.P.; Kiresuk, T.J.; and Spano, R.M. "Personality Characteristics of Women with Repeated Illegiti-macies: Descriptive Aspects." **American Journal of Orthopsy-chiatry**, 36(3): 476-484, 1966.

A sample of twenty women with repeated illegitimate pregnancies reveals that five had been incestuously abused as children and/or adolescents. A consistent pattern among these five women was that of trying to tell their mothers about the abuse and being shamed and even physically beaten for their attempted disclosures.

163. Miller, J.; Moeller, D.; Kaufman, A.; Di Vasto, P.; Pathak, D.; and Christy, J. "Recidivism Among Sex Assault Victims." **American Journal of Psychiatry**, 135(9): 1103-1104, 1978.

A sample of 341 adult female rape victims who had received services from a university-based rape crisis team contains a total of eighty-two women who had been raped on more than one occasion. Incest abuse is documented in the backgrounds of 18% of these recidivist victims who are more likely to have come from disruptive homes, have a more chaotic adult lifestyle, and are recurrently exploited financially, emotionally and sexually by others.

164. Vitaliano, P.P.; Boyer, D.; and James, J. "Percep-tions of Juvenile Experience: Females Involved in Prostitution Versus Property Offenders." **Criminal Justice and Behavior**, 8(3): 325-342, September 1981.

Eight groups of female criminals are interviewed as to their perceptions of their juvenile development. The hypo-thesis tested is that the type of criminal behavior that an adult female does for primary support is a stronger indicator of her juvenile developmental experiences than is race or socioeconomic class. It is discovered that 52% of the prosti-tutes in the groups were incestuously victimized as children, and that 59% of those incest victims had experienced serious social and/or emotional problems because of the incest. In comparison, 45% of the property offenders were incestuously abused, and 28% had experienced significant social and/or emotional problems because of the incest.

165. Yeary, J. "Incest and Chemical Dependency." **Journal of Psychoactive Drugs,** 14(1-2): 133-135, January–June 1982.

Incest is defined as abuse perpetrated on a child by a member of the child's family group and includes acts of sexual intercourse and sexual stimulation. A review of the literature reveals that incest perpetrators often have a high rate of alcoholism and that women in treatment for substance abuse report a high rate of incest in their childhoods. A case of a forty-five year old male substance abuser who had incestuously abused his daughter is presented to illustrate the contention that professionals in the substance abuse field are dealing with many clients with histories of incest victimization and/or incest-related problems.

Psychological Problems

Incest occurring in childhood and adolescence potentially disrupts the emotional development of the individual; victims, consequently, may experience emotional problems or diagnosable mental illnesses as adults. The following references examine the psychological problems often presented by female adult survivors of incest.

166. Bess, B.E. and Janssen, Y. "Incest: A Pilot Study." **Hillside Journal of Clinical Psychiatry,** 4(1): 39-52, 1982.

Thirty-two randomly selected adult female psychiatric patients are questioned as to a history of incest in their childhoods. Ten disclosed a history of incest victimization and for most of them, this was the first opportunity afforded them to talk about the incest. An examination of their backgrounds reveals that a triad of incest, parental alcoholism, and physical abuse has the most deleterious impact on adult emotional and psychosexual development.

167. Courtois, C. "The Incest Experience and Its Aftermath." **Victimology: An International Journal,** 4(4): 337-347, 1979.

A structured interview designed to elicit demographic

and family background information, as well as data on the
nature of the incest and its effect, was administered to
thirty-one female adult survivors of incest. Results indicate
that the incest variables of duration, frequency, degree
of relatedness, coercion and nondisclosure have no relationship
to the short- and longterm effects reported by the victims.
However, data also reveal that incest initiated in the prepubertal years has more severe effects on the victim, and
that victims who go through psychotherapy are more likely
to report more deleterious longterm effects than those who
do not.

168. Herman, J.L. **Father-Daughter Incest.** Cambridge,
Massachusetts: Harvard University Press, 1981.

Forty female adult survivors of incest present major
depressive symptoms, often with suicidal ideation and attempts, substance abuse, repeated sexual and physical victimization by others, and sexual dysfunctions. These incest victims
developed into archetypally feminine women: sexy without
finding pleasure in sex; repeatedly victimized yet repeatedly
overvaluing men; contemptuous of themselves and of other
women, yet nurturing and self-sacrificing.

169. Meiselman, K.C. **Incest: A Psychological Study
of Causes and Effects with Treatment Recommendations.**
San Francisco: Jossey-Bass, 1978.

Twenty-six victims of paternal incest who are psychotherapy patients are compared to fifty female psychotherapy
patients who do not report a history of incest victimization.
The incest patients average 3.4 presenting problems in therapy
while the control group averages 2.5 problems. About half
of each group was diagnosed as neurotic, and most of the
remaining patients in both groups are diagnosed as having
adjustment reactions or personality disorders. It is hypothesized that there is no association between paternal incest
and the development of any particular personality disorder
or severe psychopathology in the daughters, although incest
is clearly a source of stress that predisposes the daughters
to psychological disturbance, the precise nature of which
is largely determined by a host of environmental, individual
and genetic factors only tangentially connected to the incest.

170. Meiselman, K.C. "Personality Characteristics
of Incest History Psychotherapy Patients: A Research Note."
Archives of Sexual Behavior, 9(3): 195-197, 1980.

MMPI's were given to sixteen women in therapy for

incest-related problems and the test results are compared
to those of a control group of psychotherapy patients who
do not report a history of incest victimization and who are
matched to the victims by age, ethnicity and education.
Incest victims tend to have elevated depression, psychopathic
deviation, and schizophrenia scales, suggesting a profile
of an impulsive, delinquent, socially isolated and possibly
prepsychotic individual. Although it is tempting to label
the psychopathic deviation-schizophrenia elevations an "incest
profile," the control group shows a mean profile that is nearly
identical with the highest elevation on the psychopathic
deviation scale and a somewhat less elevated schizophrenia
scale. This study pr~sents evidence contrary to the hypothesis
that prepubertal in‿est is associated with any particular
diagnostic entity. The incest group, however, answered more
questions in the direction of sexual disturbance and it seems
plausible to assume that the incest experience is specifically
associated with adult sexual disturbances.

171. Romanik, R.L. and Goodwin, J. "Adaptation to
Pregnancy Due to Childhood Sexual Abuse." **Birth Psychology
Bulletin,** 3(2): 2-9, July 1982.

Five adult patients who disclosed a history of incest
victimization upon psychiatric referral for maladies relating
to pregnancy are described. Four had concurrent diagnoses
of adjustment reaction, schizotypal personality, Briquet's
Syndrome, and alcoholism with cyclothymic disorder. All
received brief psychotherapeutic intervention focusing on
the resolution of incest-related problems.

172. Rosenbaum, M. and Weaver, G.M. "Dissociated
State: Status of a Case After Thirty-eight Years." **Journal
of Nervous and Mental Disease,** 168(10): 597-603, October
1980.

An extensive case study of a woman psychotherapy
patient with multiple personalities and an early history of
incest victimization is presented. A literature review reveals
that of the thirty-three studies on multiple personalities
published between 1934 and 1978 in the scientific literature,
a majority involved incest victimization in the childhood
of the patients.

173. Rosenfeld, A.A. "Incidence of a History of Incest
Among Eighteen Female Psychiatric Patients." **American
Journal of Psychiatry,** 136(6): 791-795, June 1979.

Defining incest as overt sexual activity involving genital

contact between two people too closely related to marry, a history of incest victimization is elicited from all of the female patients seen in a private psychiatric practice. Six of the eighteen patients confirmed a history of incest abuse, and all are being treated for presenting problems of marital discord, sexual dysfunction, and hysterical character disorder.

174. Saltman, V. and Solomon, R.S. "Incest and Multiple Personality." **Psychological Reports,** 50(3, part 2): 1127-1141, 1982.

Multiple personalities involve the existence within the individual of two or more distinct personalities, each of which is dominant at a particular time, and each of which as a fully integrated unit has its own unique memories, behavior patterns, and social relationships. It is suggested that although there is no simple cause and effect relationship between incest and multiple personalities, there is clearly a relationship of some kind. Multiple personalities may represent a coping mechanism to deal with the guilt, rage and fear created by the incest by shifting these feelings onto alternate personalities.

175. Silver, R.L. and Boon, C. "Searching for Meaning in Misfortune: Making Sense of Incest." **Journal of Social Issues,** 39(2): 81-101, Summer 1983.

The search for meaning is an adaptive strategy in coping with an undesirable life event. Seventy-seven female adult survivors of incest were given a comprehensive questionnaire to assess the nature and extent of their search for the meaning of their incest victimization. The vast majority report a continued search for meaning and the data demonstrate that the search is unrelated to the frequency of the incestuous encounters, the physical violence involved, the age at onset, or whether the sexual contact had progressed into sexual intercourse; however, the older the woman was when the incest was terminated and the longer the incest had continued during childhood, the more intense the search for meaning. The more active the search for meaning, the more recurrent, intrusive, and disruptive thoughts about the incest are reported by the women. Also, the more active the search, the more current psychological distress is reported with a concomitant greater impairment in social functioning and a lower self-esteem. For many of the victims, the search for meaning takes the form of understanding the incest dynamics, of seeing their father as mentally ill, and of considering positive outcomes of the incest experience. For

other of the victims, however, the damage done by the incest
is so irreversible that no satisfactory meaning can be derived
from the experience.

176. Van Buskirk, S.S. and Cole, C.F. "Characteristics
of Eight Women Seeking Therapy for the Effect of Incest."
Psychotherapy: Theory, Research and Practice, 20(4): 503-514,
Winter 1983.

Eight female adult survivors of incest who were seeking
therapy for incest-related problems were given a battery
of personality and relationship surveys. Test results indicate
that the women are dissatisfied with interpersonal relationships, have difficulty in trusting, experience problems with
assertion, and have persistent feelings of vulnerability and
defenselessness.

177. Westermeyer, J. "Incest in Psychiatric Practice:
A Description of Patients and Incestuous Relationships."
Journal of Clinical Psychiatry, 39(8): 643-648, August 1978.

A sample of thirty-two psychiatric patients who report
a history of incest victimization is described. Most are experiencing sexual dysfunction; twenty are diagnosed either
as psychotic or neurotic; six have behavioral problems; and
the remaining six have psychosomatic complaints.

Psychosomatic Complaints

Many of the studies which examine the effects of
incest on adult survivors present some consideration of psychosomatic complaints. The following study focuses exclusively
on that issue.

178. Levitan, H. "Explicit Incestuous Motifs in Psychosomatic Patients." **Psychotherapy and Psychosomatics,** 37(1):
22-25, 1982.

The records of sixty-two psychosomatic patients are
compared to those of forty-eight nonpsychosomatic patients
to determine a childhood history of incest victimization.
Psychosomatic patients are significantly more likely to
report incestuous experiences. It is theorized that psychosomatic complaints may represent the failure of the ego's
defensive structure created by the incest. Four case studies
are presented to illustrate this theory.

Relationship Problems

The early betrayal of trust that occurs during incest victimization and the low self-esteem of survivors of incest often combine with a host of individual and environmental factors to interfere with the development and continuation of reciprocally satisfying relationships with others. Disturbed and strained relationships with the nuclear family are understandably quite commonly reported as well. Finally, because of the poor parenting models to which they had been exposed as children, incest victims also often express considerable doubts about their own parenting skills, as the following studies describe.

179. Abraham, K. "Neurotic Exogamy." **Psychoanalytic Review**, 8: 101-102, 1921.

The term "neurotic exogamy" is coined to describe the female incest victim's tendency to develop sexual or marriage relationships with people of other races and nationalities.

180. Herman, J.L. and Hirschman, L. "Father-Daughter Incest." **Journal of Women in Culture and Society**, 2(4): 735-756, 1977.

Fifteen female adult survivors of paternal incest demonstrate significant problems in relationships. As adults they tend to heroize and overvalue men but choose to develop relationships with abusive men. All of the women express a sense of disappointment and contempt for their fathers who had abused them, but their feelings for their mothers are even more hostile and unforgiving. Doubts about their own parenting skills are persistent and for those women who do have children, significant conflicts and even abusive behavior toward the children is often reported.

181. Herman, J.L. **Father-Daughter Incest.** Cambridge, Massachusetts: Harvard University Press, 1981.

The legacy of the childhoods of the forty female paternal incest victims in this sample is a feeling of betrayal by both parents; as a result, as adults they tend to expect abuse and disappointment in all intimate relationships, while at the same time desperately longing for nurturance and affection. A series of brief, unsatisfying relationships interspersed with periods of celibacy is the most likely way in which this conflict will be resolved. Marriage relationships are also conflictual and often characterized by physical, emotional and/or sexual violence. The majority of the victims tend to overvalue and overidealize men, and have hostile and distrustful feelings toward women. A small number of the women had experimented with lesbianism and for those who had developed a lesbian identity, this choice seems to be an adaptive and positive way of dealing with the trauma of the incest. Finally, most of the women express serious doubts about their parenting skills, and those in the sample who do have children often have conflictual and even abusive relationships with them.

182. Meiselman, K.C. **Incest: A Psychological Study of Causes and Effects with Treatment Recommendations.** San Francisco: Jossey-Bass, 1978.

Twenty-three female adult survivors of paternal incest report significant relationship problems. They tend to tolerate a great deal of abuse and rejection in interpersonal relationships, taking a "masochistic" stance which replicates the feelings of helplessness and powerlessness experienced as incest victims. Many have forgiven their fathers for the abuse, but most maintain a consistently negative and hostile attitude toward their mothers.

183. Rascovsky, M.W. and Rascovsky, A. "On Consummated Incest." **International Journal of Psychoanalysis,** 31: 42-47, 1950.

Paternal incest victims tend to seek out "father figures" in adult heterosexual relationships. One extensive case example is presented to illustrate this theory.

184. Tompkins, J.B. "Penis Envy and Incest: A Case Report." **Psychoanalytic Review,** 27: 319-325, 1940.

A case study is presented to illustrate the theory that female adult survivors of incest often unconsciously seek a "father figure" in heterosexual relationships in order to regain the positive aspects of the incest experience and to work through the emotional conflicts created by the incest.

185. Van Buskirk, S.S. and Cole, C.F. "Characteristics of Eight Women Seeking Therapy for the Effects of Incest." **Psychotherapy: Theory, Research and Practice,** 20(4): 503-514, Winter 1983.

Eight adult victims of paternal incest were administered a battery of personality and relationship surveys. All show difficulties in interpersonal relationships because of low self-esteem and an impaired ability to trust. Men like their

fathers are often sought out for sexual relationships, thereby
recreating in those relationships the feelings of helplessness
and powerlessness they had experienced as children.

Sexual Problems

Most of the studies that deal with the longterm effects
of paternal incest make reference to a wide variety of sexual
problems and dysfunctions so often experienced by adult
women who have a history of incest victimization. As the
following references demonstrate, these problems vary in
seriousness and in the extent to which they interfere with
daily functioning.

186. Herman, J.L. **Father–Daughter Incest.** Cambridge,
Massachusetts: Harvard University Press, 1981.
Over half of the forty paternal incest victims in this
sample report impairments in sexual enjoyment because
the memory of the incest victimization is intrusive, creating
"flashbacks" and uncomfortable feelings of being controlled
and dominated.

187. Hersko, M. "Incest: A Three-Way Process." **Journal
of Social Therapy,** 7: 22-31, 1966.
Female victims of paternal incest often cannot develop
sexually satisfying relationships with men as adults.

188. Meiselman, K.C. **Incest: A Psychological Study
of Causes and Effects with Treatment Recommendations.**
San Francisco: Jossey-Bass, 1978.
The most striking finding in this psychotherapy sample
of twenty-three female adult survivors of paternal incest
is the frequency of sexual problems which range from promiscuity, to frigidity, to confusion over sexual identity.

189. Meiselman, K.C. "Personality Characteristics
of Incest History Psychotherapy Patients: A Research Note."
Archives of Sexual Behavior, 9(3): 195-197, 1980.
Although the MMPI profiles of sixteen adult women
in therapy for incest-related problems are not significantly
different from the MMPI profiles of an equal number of
female therapy patients who do not report a history of incest,
the victims answered more questions in the direction of
sexual disturbance. The data would suggest that it is at
least plausible that incest victimization in childhood is specifically associated with sexual disturbances in adulthood.

190. Simari, C.G. and Baskin, D. "Incestuous Experiences within Homosexual Populations: A Preliminary Study." **Archives of Sexual Behavior,** 11(4): 329-344, August 1982.

Twenty-nine lesbians and fifty-four male homosexuals were administered a comprehensive questionnaire designed to accumulate demographic data as well as information about attitudes, personality characteristics, and life history data. Defining incest as sexual relations between genetically related individuals, it is determined that 46% of the male homosexuals had been incestuously victimized as children, and 38% of the lesbians. The use or abuse of sexual orientation as a means of coping is a defensive tactic more likely to be found in individuals whose sexual orientation is not firmly integrated. The incest experience seems to worsen an already present although largely unconscious sexual problem; it does not seem to cause it.

No Serious Effects

Some researchers have offered counterarguments and case material in support of the contention that incest has no serious repercussions for the victims. These studies range in philosophy from those which view an absence of psychosis or severe personality disorder as an indication of incest's inability to have a serious impact on the victim, while others fall into the "pro-incest" camp, asserting that the literature's concern with the effects of incest is little more than scientific hysteria.

191. Cepada, M.L. "Incest Without Harmful Repercussions." **Medical Aspects of Human Sexuality,** 12(1): 131, January 1978.

Female children with dull normal or borderline intelligence are not likely to experience serious repercussions from incest. Another group with less sequelae are adolescent females who have engaged in sustained incestuous relationship with a stepfather.

192. Henderson, D.J. "Incest: A Synthesis of Data." **Canadian Psychiatric Association Journal,** 17(4): 299-313, 1972.

A review of the literature suggests that incest is not particularly common, that girls play a collusive role in their victimization, and that the effects are not notably serious.

193. Henderson, D.J. "Is Incest Harmful?" **Canadian Journal of Psychiatry,** 28(1): 34-40, February 1983.

A critique of the scientific literature on incest demonstrates that studies are poorly done and that conclusions documenting deleterious effects of incest on the victims should be treated skeptically.

194. Rascovsky, M.W. and Rascovsky, A. "On Consummated Incest." **International Journal of Psychoanalysis,** 31: 42-47, 1950.

A case of an adult woman who had actively enjoyed her incestuous relationship with her father is presented. It is theorized that the actual consummation of the incestuous relationship diminshes the child's chances of developing psychosis later in life and allows better adjustment to the external world.

195. Schultz, L.G. "The Child Sex Victim: Social, Psychological and Legal Perspectives." **Child Welfare,** 52(3): 147-157, March 1973.

Generally, sexual assaults on children do not have excessively unsettling effects on the child's personality development nor on adult adjustment. The most damaging effects are created by the disclosure of the sexual abuse and the resultant legal and social service intervention.

196. Schultz, L.G. (Editor). **The Sexual Victimology of Youth.** Springfield, Illinois: Charles C. Thomas, Publisher, 1980.

The choice of the word "trauma" to indicate postincest effects is misleading, as is the word "victim" to indicate the status of the child. Most of the research regarding incest ends up being rhetorically manipulative and abounding in cliches and myths. The literature does not support a casual relationship between incest and any single piece of pre- or postincest behavior.

197. Yorukaglu, A. and Kemph, J.L. "Children Not Severely Damaged by Incest with a Parent." **Journal of the American Academy of Child Psychiatry,** 5: 111-124, 1966.

Two cases of incestuously abused children are presented. Although each was hospitalized in a children's psychiatric facility for anxiety, suicidal ideation, and aggressive acting out, the incest is thought to not have been severely damaging because both children maintained healthy ego functioning and did not experience psychosis.

5

Father-Son Incest

The incest taboo serves many purposes. As a biological construct, it strives to protect the species from the deleterious effects of inbreeding; as a psychosocial construct, it works to protect the family's role structure and assure the integrity of generational boundaries. Yet at the same time that the taboo is beneficial to society and to families, it has created obstacles for research: what is, in the words of Oedipus, "the last evil that can be known," has also been the last evil to be studied.

Nowhere is that more evident than with the topic of father-son incest. Although recent anonymous, self-report studies with large samples of respondents have demonstrated that the rate of the incestuous victimization of boys nearly approximates the rate for girls, and the perpetrator is invariably a male family member, studies on father-son incest are comparatively rare in the professional literature.

There are two primary reasons for the paucity of research in this area. First, role expectations that have doggedly persisted despite recent social changes have placed male victims at a decided disadvantage. The onus is too often on the male, even a male child, to resist any unwanted sexual advances, to initiate desired sexual activity, and to benefit from any sexual experience. With that expectation, the plight of victimized boys is often addressed skeptically, casually, or not at all. Second, father-son incest is often viewed as a homosexual act, not as an incestuous act, and with that perception considerations of power differences, role reversal, poor communication, and the roles of nonparticipating members that are features of an incestuous family and that combine to create victimizing experiences for the child, are often overlooked. Yet father-son incest is no more likely to be scientifically considered if viewed as a homosexual act, since like the incest taboo itself, a rampant homophobia in this society also has created obstacles for its scientific examination.

71

Most of the research on father-son incest consists of case studies, some of which are presented without a great deal of analysis. The following references describe the characteristics of the incestuous fathers.

198. Awad, G.A. "Father-Son Incest: A Case Report." **Journal of Nervous and Mental Disease,** 162(2): 135-139, February 1976.

The case of a forty-five year old father who had three incidents of sexual contact with his fourteen year old son is presented. The father had a chaotic early childhood with several foster home placements. A battery of psychological tests, including the MMPI, Rorschach, Sentence Completion, and the TAT, administered to the father reveals that he is impulsive, immature, psychologically unsophisticated, reckless without regards for the consequences, and emotionally alienated. Unconscious struggles with homosexuality are noted, as is a history of alcohol abuse.

199. de Young, M. **The Sexual Victimization of Children.** Jefferson, N.C.: McFarland, 1982.

A sample of four incestuous fathers is presented. All maintain a "heterosexual facade," despite the fact that three had repeated homosexual experiences throughout their lives. A series of rationalizations do not allow them to view the incestuous abuse of their sons as homosexual in nature. All four of the fathers were sexually abused themselves as children, each by an older male. Character disorders are diagnosed for two of the fathers; the remaining two are free from any diagnosable mental illness. None of the fathers is alcoholic.

200. Dixon, K.N.; Arnold, L.E.; and Calestro, K. "Father-Son Incest: Underreported Psychiatric Problem?" **American Journal of Psychiatry,** 135(7): 835-838, July 1978.

Six cases of father-son incest which came to the attention of a psychiatric clinic are described in detail. Each of the fathers has a history of sociopathy and/or alcoholism, and has marked problems with judgment and impulse control. None of the fathers reports homosexual experiences prior to the incestuous abuse of his son. Parallels to the individual and family dynamics of father-daughter incest are noted, suggesting that the sex of the parent is a more important variable in incest than the sex of the child.

201. Edwards, N.B. "Case Conference: Assertive Training

in a Case of Homosexual Pedophilia." **Journal of Behavior Therapy and Experimental Psychiatry**, 3: 55–63, 1972.

Assertiveness training and thought-stopping techniques bring about significant positive changes in the behavior of a father who incestuously abused his three sons.

202. Langsley, D.G.; Schwartz, M.N.; and Fairbairn, R.H. "Father-Son Incest." **Comprehensive Psychiatry**, 9(3): 218–226, May 1968.

An extensive case history of homosexual incest in two generations of a family is presented. The abusive father grew up in a religiously conservative family in a small town and was taught that sex was evil. He had homosexual experiences with a young uncle at the age of twelve and with a cousin at the age of twenty-five; and during adolescence he fell in love with an eight year old boy after whom he later named his son. Occupationally successful and perceived as a good family man, he continued to struggle with homosexual impulses and developed an incestuous relationship with his son that lasted eighteen months. His son disclosed the incest at age twenty while being treated for a psychotic reaction to LSD.

203. Medlicott, R.W. "Parent-Child Incest." **Australia and New Zealand Journal of Psychiatry**, 1: 180–187, 1967.

A sample of three cases of father-son incest is presented. All of the fathers are occupationally successful and none is psychotic. All deny having homosexual experiences or impulses.

204. Meiselman, K.C. **Incest: A Psychological Study of Causes and Effects with Treatment Recommendations.** San Francisco: Jossey-Bass, 1978.

A psychotherapy sample of incest victims contains two cases of father-son incest which are described in detail. In both cases the sexual activity was initiated by the fathers, both of whom had experienced strong homosexual urges throughout their lives. The sons did not resist and experienced some curiosity and fascination about the incest initiated by the fathers to whom they were strongly emotionally bonded.

205. Raybin, J.B. "Homosexual Incest." **Journal of Nervous and Mental Disease**, 148: 105–109, 1969.

Homosexual incest in two generations of a family is described. The father initiated an incestuous act with his adolescent son. As a child, the father had been incestuously victimized by his son's grandfather, a family patriarch and

pillar of the community who had never been known to have
acted out homosexually outside of the family. Stimulated
by the incest, the father engaged in a long incestuous relationship with a younger brother and with a male cousin; as an
adult, despite his heterosexual facade, he maintained a series
of homosexual affairs. His son experienced a psychotic break
after the initiation of the incest.

Mothers of Incestuously Victimized Sons

Little is known about the role that the nonparticipating
mother plays in father-son incest, or about the nature of
the incestuous family as a system. What information is avail-
able is generally derived from the case studies of father-son
incest.

206. Awad, G.A. "Father-Son Incest: A Case Report."
Journal of Nervous and Mental Disease, 162(2): 135-139,
February 1976.
The nonparticipating mother in the presented case
of an incestuous father is described as having vehemently
denied the reality of the incest. Prior to the overt incest,
the marriage relationship of the couple had deteriorated
significantly.

207. de Young, M. **The Sexual Victimization of Children.**
Jefferson, N.C.: McFarland, 1982.
The wives of two incestuous fathers in a sample of
four were interviewed. Each was aware that the incest was
occurring but an extensive rationalization system deterred
them from intervening. In unhappy and unfulfilling marriages,
they experienced secondary gains from their husbands' victimi-
zations of their sons, and played unconsciously collusive
roles in the initiation and continuation of the incest.

208. Dixon, K.N.; Arnold, L.E.; and Calestro, K. "Father-
Son Incest: Underreported Psychiatric Problem?" **American
Journal of Psychiatry,** 135(7): 835-838, July 1978.
The wives of the six incestuous fathers in the sample
appear to be overwhelmed with family responsibilities and
largely unable to exercise protective coping skills. Each
played a collusive role in the initiation and continuation
of her husband's incestuous victimization of their son.

Effects on the Son

The son who is a paternal incest victim bears a double stigma: he is not only a victim of incest, he is also a participant in a homosexual relationship. References to the effects of incest on males are sparse in the literature. Some combine victimized boys with girls in samples of paternal incest victims and deal with the effects on the children in general with no suggestion that they may be gender specific. Others, especially those that take the case study approach, describe the effects of the paternal incest on the sons of the fathers in their sample, and that data may be generalized to other cases. For the sake of convenience, the effects will be categorized according to the developmental stage of the son.

Effects on Children

The effects of paternal incest on prepubertal boys are described in the following references.

209. Adams-Tucker, C. "Proximate Effects of Sexual Abuse in Childhood: A Report on Twenty-Eight Children." **American Journal of Psychiatry,** 139(10): 1252-1256, October 1982.

Six boys are part of a sample of twenty-eight sexually molested children who range in age from $2\frac{1}{2}$ to $15\frac{1}{2}$; most were incestuously victimized by their fathers. The Louisville Behavior Checklist Test results indicate that the children are all symptomatic in one or more of the following areas: self-destructive, suicidal and/or withdrawing behavior; sexual complaints, running away, and/or aggressive behavior; school, peer and/or parent problems; and anxiety, psychosomatic, and/or sleep-related problems. The emotional disturbance suffered by the victims is most severe when the sexual abuse begins at an early age and continues repetitively over a long period of time; or when it begins in the adolescent years, even though its frequency and duration may be limited. All of the subjects experience emotional and behavioral problems as serious as those of children seeking psychiatric help for any other reason.

210. Bender, L. and Blau, A. "The Reactions of Children to Sexual Relationships with Adults." **American Journal of Orthopsychiatry,** 7: 500-518, 1937.

In this sample of sexually victimized children, there

is one case of a six year old boy who was incestuously abused by his father. Stimulated by the activity, the boy then initiated an incestuous relationship with his younger sister. Upon psychiatric referral, the boy is found to be of normal intelligence, but experiencing confusion about role relationships in the family and feelings of resentment and anger towards his father.

211. Dixon, K.N.; Arnold, L.E.; and Calestro, K. "Father-Son Incest: Underreported Psychiatric Problem?" **American Journal of Psychiatry,** 135(7): 835–838, July 1977.

The six sons victimized by paternal incest have intense, even homicidal, wishes against their fathers. Four of the sons have suicidal ideation; three engage in self-destructive and/or self-injuring behaviors. Although none is psychotic, all experience severe behavioral problems.

212. Emslie, G.J. and Rosenfeld, A.A. "Incest Reported by Children and Adolescents Hospitalized for Severe Psychiatric Problems." **American Journal of Psychiatry,** 140(6): 708–711, June 1983.

Sixty-five male and female children who are hospitalized for severe psychiatric problems are the subjects of this study. Incest victimization is discovered in the early childhood of 8% of the twenty-five boys. The single factor common to children and adolescents who suffer from serious psychopathology that requires psychiatric hospitalization is severe family disorganization and the ego impairment it creates, whether or not it is accompanied by incest.

213. Thomas, J.N. "Yes, You Can Help a Sexually Abused Child." **RN,** 43(8): 23–29, August 1980.

On the basis of the medical examinations of 500 sexually abused children, two hundred of whom are incest victims and fifty of whom are boys, the following symptoms are most commonly noted: venereal disease; rectal pain, swelling or bleeding; behavioral disturbances such as sudden irritability, regressive behavior, and decline in the quality of school performance; and behavioral problems such as running away from home, drug abuse, excessive masturbation, and sexually precocious behavior and comments.

Effects on Adolescents

The adolescent boy's reactions to paternal incest are likely to be played out in the public arena. Allowed more

freedom and given encouragement by role expectations
that support adolescent acting out in general, and acting
out in boys in specific, the male incest victim often experiences a wide variety of behavioral, emotional and sexual identity
problems.

214. Justice, B. and Justice, R. **The Broken Taboo.**
New York: Human Sciences Press, 1979.

A boy who is sexually abused by his father has to cope
with the stress of role reversal and the threat to his masculinity that the incest represents. Adolescent boys usually
experience overwhelming anxiety and marked conflicts over
their sexual identity, frequently using drugs or turning to
prostitution as ways of coping with these feelings.

215. Nasjleti, M. "Suffering in Silence: The Male Incest
Victim." **Child Welfare,** 49(5): 269-275, May 1980.

Nine male victims of parental incest, ranging in age
from 12 to 17, show a consistent pattern of extreme resistance
to describing their molestation experiences in a group therapy
setting. Clinging to the cultural concept of masculinity
that emphasizes aggressiveness, non-dependence, non-nurturance, and physical strength, the boys who were molested
by their fathers have fears concerning homosexuality and
mental illness. Those fears, coupled with their shame at
not having been the dominant person controlling the molestation experience, create a marked resistance to reporting
and discussing the incest.

216. Rhinehart, J.W. "Genesis of Overt Incest." **Comprehensive Psychiatry,** 2: 338-349, 1961.

The case of an eighteen year old male patient who
behaved effeminantly and expressed a desire to be a woman
is discussed. The young man was a victim of incest perpetrated
by his alcoholic father and later by an older brother.

217. Saffer, J.B.; Sanson, P.; and Gentry, J. "The Awe-
some Burden Upon the Child Who Must Keep a Family Secret."
Child Psychiatry and Human Development, 10(1): 35-40,
Fall 1979.

The case of a seventeen year old boy with dysphoria,
chronic fatigue, slowed responses, lack of interest, mild
anorexia, and suicidal ideation is presented. The young man
had been incestuously victimized by his father who had threat-
ened to send him to a foster home if he disclosed the incest.

Effects on Adults

The greatest impact, although certainly not the sole impact, of father-son incest seems to be on the development of the sexual identity of the victim. The almost exclusive focus of studies on this effect at least partially may reflect a culturally conditioned concern about male sex roles, particularly as they pertain to adult males.

218. Berry, G.W. "Incest: Some Clinical Variations on a Classical Theme." **Journal of the American Academy of Psychoanalysis,** 3: 151-161, 1975.

The case of a twenty-four year old nonpsychotic male who sought therapy because of a limited ability to enjoy heterosexual relationships is presented. The man was incestuously abused by his father during his adolescence.

219. de Young, M. **The Sexual Victimization of Children.** Jefferson, N.C.: McFarland, 1982.

Six sons, incestuously abused by their fathers, demonstrate self-destructive acting out during their adolescence and adulthood. Diagnosable mental illness is not a feature of the sample, but all of the sons have fears about homosexuality, although none of them has engaged in a homosexual relationship outside of the incest with his father.

220. Medlicott, R.W. "Parent-Child Incest." **Australia and New Zealand Journal of Psychiatry,** 1: 180-187, 1967.

Three sons, incestuously abused by their fathers, experience significant psychological problems as adults. Two are chronically neurotic, and one had a psychotic break over his fears about becoming a homosexual and then committed suicide.

221. Meiselman, K.C. **Incest: A Psychological Study of Causes and Effects with Treatment Recommendations.** San Francisco: Jossey-Bass, 1978.

Two adult males who had experienced incest with their fathers sought psychotherapy for incest-related problems. One of the subjects had episodes of severe depression exacerbated by alcohol abuse. The other, an intelligent and highly motivated college student, was struggling with a bisexual identity.

222. Saltman, V. and Solomon, R.S. "Incest and the Multiple Personality." **Psychological Reports,** 50(3, part 2): 1127-1141, 1982.

Six cases of multiple personality, one of which is an adult male, are described. Multiple personalities involve the existence within the individual of two or more distinct personalities, each of which is dominant at a particular time, and each of which as a fully integrated unit has its own unique memories, behavioral patterns, and social relationships. It is suggested that although there is no simple cause and effect relationship between incest and multiple personalities, there is clearly a relationship of some kind. Multiple personalities may represent a coping mechanism to deal with the guilt, rage and fear created by the incest by shifting these feelings into alternate personalities.

223. Simori, C.G. and Baskin, D. "Incestuous Experiences Within Homosexual Populations: A Preliminary Study." **Archives of Sexual Behavior,** 11(4): 329-344, August 1982.

Twenty-nine lesbians and fifty-four male homosexuals were administered a comprehensive questionnaire designed to elicit demographic data as well as information about attitudes, personality characteristics, and life history information. Defining incest as sexual relations between genetically related individuals, it is determined that 46% of the male homosexuals had been incestuously victimized as children, and 38% of the lesbians. The use or abuse of sexual orientation as a means of coping is a defensive tactic more likely to be found in individuals whose sexual orientation is not firmly integrated. The incest experience seems to worsen an already present although largely unconscious sexual problem; it does not seem to cause it.

224. Swift, C. "The Prevention of Sexual Child Abuse: Focus on the Perpetrator." **Journal of Clinical Child Psychology,** 8(2): 133-136, Summer 1979.

The prevention of child sexual abuse begins with understanding two things about the offenders: they usually have experienced sexual abuse themselves as children, and they are sexually ignorant. Case studies and references from the literature support these two hypotheses. Prevention, then, must incorporate prompt therapeutic intervention with sexually molested boys, and public education about sex in general and sexual abuse in particular.

6

Sibling Incest

Researchers are in general agreement that sibling incest is the most prevalent type of incest behavior. The literature, however, does not always clearly distinguish, or in some references even acknowledge, the qualitative difference between a sibling who uses his or her advanced age, maturity, or psychosexual development to coerce, manipulate, or otherwise inveigle another sibling into engaging in a sexual act, and two or more siblings who participate in a mutually agreed upon, reciprocally satisfying sexual encounter which is exploratory and experimental in nature.

The failure to recognize that difference has created scientific support for a general social apathy about sibling incest. The topic evokes little ire so that the taboo against the behavior is quite relaxed; with the possible exception of the most obviously abusive cases, few incidents are reported to authorities by parents who prefer to handle the situation within the family and without outside intervention. Those factors, in turn, combine to produce few reported cases for study by researchers and comparatively few references to sibling incest in the professional literature.

Rate of Occurrence

Speculations about the rate of occurrence of sibling incest range from projections based upon clinical experience to more sophisticated estimates derived from large samples of respondents. Since there is a general consensus that sibling incest is much more prevalent than any other type of incest, theories about the origin, nature, and restraining power of the sibling incest taboo are also found in the literature.

225. Arndt, W.B. and Ladd, B. "Sibling Incest Aversion as an Index of Oedipal Conflict." **Journal of Personality Assessment**, 45(1): 52-58, February 1981.

The most notable residue of the Oedipal conflict as it is described in psychoanalytic literature is the incest taboo; one way to measure the intensity of that conflict, then, is to assess the degree of incest aversion. A thirty-item sibling incest aversion scale was designed and administered to fifty-three male and fifty female college students. Using a five point rating scale with one indicating strongly agree and five indicating strongly disagree, the mean sibling incest aversion score for males is 113.64, and 123.54 for females. Data analysis reveals that male respondents who have a sister express significantly more aversion to sibling incest than those who do not; female respondents with a strong aversion to sibling incest tend to be sexually inhibited in general, while those with low aversion are more liberal in their sexual attitudes and behaviors. The findings demonstrate a relationship between incest aversion, hostility guilt, neuroticism, extraversion, and sensitization for females, although significant results for males are not documented. It is suggested that the sibling incest aversion scale is a useful construct for assessing the intensity of the Oedipal conflict.

226. Finkelhor, D. "Sex Among Siblings: A Survey on Prevalence, Variety and Effects." **Archives of Sexual Behavior**, 9(3): 171-194, June 1980.

A survey with questions about childhood sexual experiences with adults and children, incestuous sexual experiences and coercive sexual experiences at any age was administered to 796 New England college and university students. Of the 530 female respondents, 15% report sibling incest experiences, while 10% of the 266 males also report sibling incest experiences. It is hypothesized that these figures almost certainly underestimate the rate of occurrence, since some respondents concealed their experiences because of guilt and shame, while others simply forgot about them. Most of the experiences were reported to have occurred when the respondents were between the ages of eight and eleven years, and that age range suggests that the experiences are not sexual play in nature. Sexual activity between siblings tends to resemble sexual activities between children in general, with a great deal of fondling and exposure; sexual intercourse or attempted sexual intercourse is rare. Approximately 25% of the respondents report that force or physical coercion accompanied the incest.

227. Lester, D. "Incest." **Journal of Sex Research**, 8(4): 268-285, 1972.

Using Kinsey Group data, it is estimated that the rate
of occurrence of sibling incest is five times higher than
that of paternal incest.

228. Lindzey, G. "Some Remarks Concerning Incest,
the Incest Taboo, and Psychoanalytic Theory." **American
Psychologist**, 22(12): 1051-1059, December 1967.

Using Kinsey Group data, it is estimated that the rate
of occurrence of sibling incest is five times higher than
that of paternal incest.

229. Lumsden, C.J. and Wilson, E.O. "Gene-Culture
Translation in the Avoidance of Sibling Incest." **Proceedings
of the National Academy of Science**, 77(10): 6248-6250,
October 1980.

A preliminary analysis is made of the relationship
between the epigenetic rules of brother-sister incest avoidance
which operate during individual development, and the frequency of occurrence of this form of incest among cultures.

Family Setting of Sibling Incest

The family environment in which sibling incest occurs
is no less important a variable than it is in considerations
of paternal incest. That sex between siblings does occur
at all, and that it occurs frequently over considerable lengths
of time in many cases, suggests that family roles, communication patterns, and the exercise of intrafamilial power may
for whatever reasons be impaired in these families. Only
a few references in the literature, however, have explored
to any extent the family setting of sibling incest.

230. de Young, M. **The Sexual Victimization of Children**.
Jefferson, N.C.: McFarland, 1982.

In a clinical sample of five cases of sibling incest,
the nature of the family is an important variable. Three
of the fathers of the siblings in the sample are absent from
the family due to death, separation, or incapacitation by
mental illness; the remaining two fathers are "emotionally
absent," having little affective investment in the lives of
their children. The mothers are passive and ineffectual,
and largely unable to supervise their children. Attitudes
about sex in these five families tend to be puritanical and
rigid, and may have had a paradoxic effect on the children.

In two of the cases, paternal incest with the female children preceded the sibling incest, suggesting that the sons may have imitated their fathers' behavior and may have seen their sisters as "spoiled goods," undeserving of their care and protection.

231. Eist, H.I. and Mandel, A.U. "Family Treatment of Ongoing Incest Behavior." **Family Process,** 7(2): 216-232, September 1968.
The treatment approach taken with one incestuous family is described. Paternal incest had preceded the sibling incest in this family.

232. Magal, V. and Winnick, H.Z. "Role of Incest in Family Structure." **Israel Annals of Psychiatry and Related Disciplines,** 6: 173-189, 1968.
All of the five incestuous families in treatment in a psychiatric facility in Israel are dysfunctional. In all of the cases, paternal incest preceded the sibling incest.

233. Meiselman, K.C. **Incest: A Psychological Study of Causes and Effects with Treatment Recommendations.** San Francisco: Jossey-Bass, 1978.
Eight cases of sibling incest are presented. The most consistent finding with regard to the family setting is that the children lack parental supervision. The youngest sister in a larger family with several older brothers is especially vulnerable to sibling incest. In approximately one-half of the cases examined, the father is dead, or is incapacitated by mental illness or alcoholism; in three of the cases, the mother is dead and had been replaced with a stepmother or adoptive mother who was never able to form a strong maternal bond with the children. Rigid and puritanical attitudes about sex are common in these families, although in one case, paternal incest had preceded the sibling incest.

234. Raphling, D.L.; Carpenter, B.L.; and Davis, A. "Incest: A Geneological Study." **Archives of General Psychiatry,** 16: 505-511, 1967.
The social learning model of incest is illustrated by a case study of a family in which incest has occurred in three generations. In this family, paternal incest preceded the sibling incest. The father had had sex with his daughter and then had encouraged his son to do so, apparently in an attempt to recreate his own early childhood experiences.

235. Weinberg, S.K. **Incest Behavior.** New York: Citadel, 1955.

In cases of sibling incest, the father fails to serve as a "restraining agent" in the family. Loose sex cultures in these families are also common, with obscenities, pornography, and nudity tolerated and openly displayed. Sibling incest is often preceded by paternal incest so that the children become prematurely sexually stimulated.

The Brothers

Most cases of sibling incest described in the literature place the responsibility for the initiation of the incest on the brother. Frequently older and more psychosexually mature, he has other characteristics that are important variables in determining the nature of the incest victimization and the effects it may have on the participants, as the following references demonstrate.

236. de Young, M. **The Sexual Victimization of Children.** Jefferson, N.C.: McFarland, 1982.

In this sample of five cases of sibling incest, the brothers had assumed the "little father" role in the family. Older than their sisters, the brothers are described as demanding, argumentative and coercive in the exercise of power created by this role reversal. Two of the brothers also had molested children outside of the family, in each case, girls close in age to their sisters, suggesting some displacement of aggressive and sexual impulses. In two of the cases, the sibling incest clearly evolved out of consensual sex play; in two other cases, it may have represented an attempt to replicate the paternal incest that had preceded it. Mutual collusion between the siblings keeps the incest secret, and if disclosure does occur, it is usually by the sister and frequently in retaliation for something the brother had done.

237. Kubo, S. "Researches and Studies of Incest in Japan." **Hiroshima Journal of Medical Sciences,** 8: 99–159, 1959.

Thirteen cases of brother–sister incest are examined. In most of the cases, the father of the family was absent or incapacitated and the brother had assumed the father's role in the family. None of the brothers in this sample appears to be mentally ill.

238. Meiselman, K.C. **Incest: A Psychological Study of Causes and Effects with Treatment Recommendations.** San Francisco: Jossey-Bass, 1978.

In the eight cases of sibling incest in this psychotherapy sample, the incestuous brothers are described by their sisters as "bullies" who teased them and liked to demonstrate their superior physical strength. Only one of the brothers clearly was psychologically disturbed at the time of the incest; and in another case, the sibling incest represented the brother's attempt to defend against homosexual impulses. In three of the cases, the incest developed out of mutual sexually exploratory play; in the other cases, it was initiated by the brothers, two of whom raped their sisters. Sexual intercourse or attempted sexual intercourse occurred in half of the cases.

239. Weinberg, S.K. **Incest Behavior.** New York: Citadel, 1955.

Most incestuous brothers are of normal intelligence. Although some have engaged in acts of juvenile delinquency, most show better personal and social adjustment than do incestuous fathers.

The Sisters

Females invariably describe early sexual experiences in more negative terms than do males. Cultural and sex role conditioning is more likely to render them passive participants in sexual encounters and victims in incestuous experiences. The following references examine the characteristics of the sisters in sibling incest.

240. de Young, M. **The Sexual Victimization of Children.** Jefferson, N.C.: McFarland, 1982.

A sample of five sisters who had engaged in sibling incest reveals that two of them had been sexually molested by males outside of the family subsequent to their first incestuous encounters with their brothers. Two of the sisters also had been incestuously abused by their father prior to the sibling incest. This data suggest that sisters in sibling incest may lack protective coping skills and that the incest is a prelude to a lifelong history of vulnerability to victimization. Only one of the sisters in the sample is of lower than average intelligence.

241. Meiselman, K.C. **Incest: A Psychological Study of Causes and Effects with Treatment Recommendations.** San Francisco: Jossey-Bass, 1978.

In a psychotherapy sample of eight sisters who had participated in sibling incest, two are found to be of below average intelligence. Aside from that finding, no significant characteristics of the sisters are noted.

242. Weinberg, S.K. **Incest Behavior.** New York: Citadel, 1955.

Adolescent sisters involved in sibling incest are more likely to have been sexually promiscuous before the sibling incest began, and those sisters were more likely to have initiated the incest. Lower intelligence is also found more often in these sisters than with other female incest victims.

Effects of Sibling Incest

Because of the frequently less coercive, more reciprocally satisfying nature of sibling incest, and because of the more collusive nature of the secret-keeping and the lesser fear that disclosure will disrupt or destroy the family, the effects of sibling incest are generally less deleterious on the participants. Caution must be taken not to generalize too widely, however, since recent studies on sibling incest have demonstrated that previously unreported longterm effects may be found in samples of sibling incest participants.

243. de Young, M. **The Sexual Victimization of Children.** Jefferson, N.C.: McFarland, 1982.

Quite a few of the sibling incest participants in this sample of five describe the experience as pleasurable; negative effects are most often reported by those who had experienced aggression, threats, or coercion during the course of the incest. All of the participants in this sample are young, so longterm effects could not be assessed. Each disclosed the incest, although none to a parent, and the disclosure seemed to increase what was an already alarming amount of parent-child alienation. Strains in the sibling relationship were also noted after the disclosure, but seemed to heal quite quickly.

244. Finkelhor, D. "Sex Among Siblings: A Survey of Prevalence, Variety and Effects." **Archives of Sexual Behavior,** 9(3): 171-194, June 1980.

A survey with questions about childhood sexual experiences with adults and children, incestuous sexual experiences, and coercive sexual experiences at any age was administered to 796 New England college and university students. Regression analysis of data show that age difference is the most significant factor in the participants' responses to the incest: the larger the age difference between the siblings, the more negatively the experience was perceived, especially by the younger siblings. A crucial developmental task in adolescence and young adulthood is learning to combine friendship with sex, and with the use of the Sexual Self-Esteem Index, there is some evidence to suggest that female participants in sibling incest may have an advantage in accomplishing that task over females who had never experienced sibling incest. For males, however, sibling sexual experiences may be associated with lower sexual self-esteem because males are the initiators of sex more often, so in those cases in which sibling sex is an outgrowth of sexual maladjustment, the pathology is more likely to reside in the male. On the whole, the evidence weighs against an extremely alarmist view of sibling incest.

245. Gebhard, P.H.; Gagnon, J.H.; Pomeroy, W.; and Christenson, C. **Sex Offenders: An Analysis of Types.** New York: Harper and Row, 1965.

Incarcerated incest offenders, rapists and homosexual offenders are compared to incarcerated non-sexual offenders and a nonincarcerated control group as to childhood experiences with sibling incest. Of the homosexual offenders, 3% report having had an incestuous relationship with a sister; 3.5% of the incest offenders report sibling incest during their childhood; and 4.5% of the rapists. Disclosures of sibling incest are made by 1.7% of the incarcerated non-sexual offenders, and by .2% of the control group.

246. Greenland, C. "Incest." **British Journal of Delinquency,** 9: 62–65, 1958.

Aversion to sex may be one of the longterm effects of sibling incest.

247. Kubo, S. "Researches and Studies of Incest in Japan." **Hiroshima Journal of Medical Sciences,** 8: 99–159, 1959.

Less negative longterm effects of sibling incest are noted in the thirteen cases in this sample when they are

compared to cases of paternal incest. A few of the sisters
show sexual promiscuity, and one is mentally ill.

248. Lukianowicz, N. "Incest I: Paternal Incest; Incest
II: Other Types of Incest." **British Journal of Psychiatry,**
120(556): 301-313, March 1972.
No "ill effects" are noted in this small sample of adolescent girls who had been incestuously victimized by their
brothers.

249. Magal, V. and Winnick, H.Z. "Role of Incest in
Family Structure." **Israel Annals of Psychiatry and Related
Disciplines,** 6: 173-189, 1968.
Averson to sex may be one of the longterm effects
of sibling incest.

250. Meiselman, K.C. **Incest: A Psychological Study
of Causes and Effects with Treatment Recommendations.**
San Francisco: Jossey-Bass, 1978.
In the psychotherapy sample of eight cases of sibling
incest retrospectively reported by adults, three of the participants are diagnosed as mentally ill. All of those over the
age of eighteen have been married at least once, and that
fact coupled with other data suggests that these subjects
are less conflicted about entering into heterosexual relationships than are the victims of paternal incest. Those subjects
with male children show an extreme difficulty in relating
to their sons, perhaps because they are displacing on them
the feelings they have for their brothers. Mild sexual adjustment problems are also noted, and four of the eight subjects
had been raped by men not related to them during their
adolescence or adulthood.

251. Sloane, P. and Karpinsky, E. "Effects of Incest
on the Participants." **American Journal of Orthopsychiatry,**
12(4): 666-673, October 1942.
Two cases of sibling incest are presented. Females
involved in sibling incest often become promiscuous. Although
each subject will react to the incest in her own way, depending
upon her predisposition and her ego and superego strengths,
both of the subjects in the sample tend to be compulsive,
delinquent, and have a hysterical personality disorder.

252. Weinberg, S.K. **Incest Behavior.** New York: Citadel,
1955.
The most commonly noted longterm effect of sibling
incest is sexual promiscuity in the female participant.

Brother–Brother Incest

Only a few references in the literature can be found on brother–brother incest.

253. Meiselman, K.C. **Incest: A Psychological Study of Causes and Effects with Treatment Recommendations.** San Francisco: Jossey-Bass, 1978.
One case of brother–brother incest is found in a psychotherapy sample. He had been anally raped at the age of ten by his fifteen year old stepbrother. Telling no one about the incident, he entered into psychotherapy for sexual problems related to a series of brief, unfulfilling extramarital affairs, which are viewed as a compulsive attempt to prove his masculinity because of incest-induced fears of being homosexual.

254. Raybin, J.B. "Homosexual Incest." **Journal of Nervous and Mental Disease,** 148: 105–109, 1969.
Homosexual incest in two generations of a family is discussed. The father initiated an incestuous act with his adolescent son. As a child, the father had been incestuously abused by his son's grandfather; stimulated by the incest, he had then engaged in a long incestuous affair with his brother.

255. Rhinehart, J.W. "Genesis of Overt Incest." **Comprehensive Psychiatry,** 2: 338–349, 1961.
The case of an eighteen year old male psychiatric patient who behaved effeminantly and expressed a desire to be a woman is discussed. The young man was a victim of incest perpetrated by his alcoholic father and later by an older brother.

7

Maternal Incest

Researchers generally have agreed that mother-child incest is a rare phenomenon, a curious consensus in light of the fact that the literature is rife with case examples and theoretical speculations about the etiology of this apparently unusual form of incest. Perhaps it is the very fact that it is uncommon that draws attention to it; perhaps it is also what appears to be the flagrant violation of rigid role expectations for the behavior of women as mothers that entices researchers to explore this type of incest.

Regardless of the motivation behind the scientific inquiry into maternal incest, the consensus remains that it is a very rare form of child sexual abuse. Only one reference in the professional literature offers a thorough analysis as to why mothers seem to be disinclined to engage in incestuous behavior with their children.

256. Finkelhor, D. **Sexually Victimized Children.** New York: The Free Press, 1979.

A survey with questions about childhood sexual experiences with adults and children, incestuous sexual experiences, and coercive sexual experiences at any age was administered to 796 New England college and university students. Fifteen report childhood sexual experiences of any kind with a female; one of those respondents had been sexually abused by her mother. Several facets of the relationship between women and children in general are possible explanations for the female reticence about engaging in sex with children. First, women have more physical contact with children and are less inhibited and self-conscious in that contact since it is both sanctioned and accepted by society. Second, women have more involvement with genital and excretory functions of children, and that involvement reduces their fascination and fantasy about them, thereby diffusing some of the sexual tension that may occur in interactions with children. Third, women also have more direct responsibility for the care

91

of children, and the protection of their well-being that that care creates may render them more sensitive to the trauma that can be created by the sexual abuse of children. Fourth, socially conditioned channels of sexual attraction draw women away from children, but draw men towards them. Women are more likely to choose their sexual partners from men older than themselves, while men choose partners from younger women. Finally, mutuality as a foundation for sexual involvement is emphasized more by women, while men are more inclined to emphasize gratification as an end to itself.

Mother-Son Incest

The psychoanalytic theory emphasis on the latent incestuous wishes between mothers and sons which must be resolved during the Oedipal stage of personality development has drawn scientific attention to cases in which that normal developmental process has been subverted by maternal incest. Although acknowledged to be extremely rare and strongly prohibited by taboo, those cases of mother-son incest have garnered scientific scrutiny greatly out of proportion to their alleged rate of occurrence.

One of the interesting themes that emerges from these references is that serious psychopathology seems to rest with the participant who initiates the incest. While father-daughter incest is generally coercive in nature and acted out against the will of the child, the initiator of mother-son incest may be the son, and in those cases in which that is true, he is invariably described as severely mentally ill. Conversely, when the mother initiates the incest, she is usually portrayed as more disturbed than her son who is then likely to later develop serious psychopathology as a consequence of the incest. As a result of this theme, the consideration of who was responsible for the initiation of the incest joins the variables of the type of sexual abuse, the degree of coercion, and the frequency and the duration in defining the nature of the incestuous experience and its impact on the son.

Characteristics of Incestuous Mothers

The following references describe the characteristics of the incestuous mothers in cases of mother-son incest. The roles of nonparticipating family members and the nature of the family system are also presented if they are discussed in the references.

257. de Young, M. **The Sexual Victimization of Children.** Jefferson, N.C.: McFarland, 1982.

Two mothers who initiated incest with their sons are described. Both of the women had been raised in chaotic families characterized by economic deprivation, frequent moves, the multiple marriages of their mothers, and sexual victimization. Both married young to men who were disinterested in child rearing and largely uninvolved in the emotional lives of their families. Each of the husbands knew about the incestuous victimization of their sons but lacked both the intrafamilial power and the emotional interest to intercede, rationalizing that their sons were simply experiencing a necessary, albeit unusual, introduction to sexual behavior. In response to their husbands' emotional withdrawal from the family, the mothers developed extremely dependent relationships with their sons, perceiving them as mates rather than as children. Overt incest in these two cases evolved slowly over time and perhaps because of the social isolation of these two families, the mothers exerted little pressure on their sons to keep the incest secret. Neither of the mothers is an alcoholic or drug abuser; both are diagnostically mentally ill. It is hypothesized that the incest, in part, may represent a repetition compulsion in which the mothers attempted to deal with the trauma of their own sexual victimization by recreating victimizing experiences.

258. Finch, S.M. "Sexual Abuse by Mothers." **Medical Aspects of Human Sexuality,** 7(1): 191, January 1973.

Incestuously abusive mothers have low self-esteem, a history of premarital and extramarital promiscuity, alcohol abuse and mental illness.

259. Forward, S. and Buck, C. **Betrayal of Innocence: Incest and Its Devastation.** Los Angeles, California: J.P. Tarcher, Inc., 1978.

In cases of mother-son incest, the mother is highly dependent and maneuvers her son into the role of the "little father" in the family. In the vast majority of cases, the father is absent from the home or is incapacitated so that he cannot play a significant role in the family system.

260. Frances, V. and Frances, A. "The Incest Taboo and Family Structure." **Family Process,** 15(2): 235-244, June 1976.

In those rare families in which mother-son incest is actually consummated, either or both participants are almost always psychotic. Roles in these families invariably are unclear and frequently reversed, and generational boundaries are blurred.

261. Justice, B. and Justice, R. **The Broken Taboo.** New York: Human Sciences Press, 1979.

Mothers who commit incest with their sons are motivated by the same reasons as fathers who incestuously abuse their daughters. Role reversals, social isolation, jealousy and possessiveness are frequently found in these families, and the incestuous mothers are often promiscuous and mentally ill.

262. Meiselman, K.C. **Incest: A Psychological Study of Causes and Effects with Treatment Recommendations.** San Francisco: Jossey-Bass, 1978.

In the psychotherapy sample of fifty-eight incest victims, there are two cases of mother-son incest. In one case, the mother who had initiated the incest is described as having a parenting style that vacillated between overprotection and physical abuse. She developed a seductive relationship with her son and often confided in him about her unfulfilling relationship with his father. The incest progressed slowly over time from fondling to sexual intercourse. In the second case, the mother, a psychotic and alcoholic prostitute, sexually and physically abused her son and forced him to witness her sexual acts with her customers.

263. Wahl, C.M. "The Psychodynamics of Consummated Maternal Incest." **Archives of General Psychiatry,** 3(2): 188-193, August 1960.

Two cases of maternal incest, one initiated by the mother and the other by the son, are presented in detail. In the first case, the mother was an attractive and provocative woman who had a controlling style in the family. She had been married five times. In the second case, the mother was promiscuous and a chronic alcoholic who was separated from her husband. Psychodynamics likely to be encountered in cases of maternal incest include the absence of a strong father figure in the home, the loss of maternal control through alcohol abuse, the son's early witnessing of the primal scene, and the son's sexual experiences with many different family members while the maternal incest is occurring.

264. Yorukaglu, A. and Kemph, J.P. "Children Not
Severely Damaged by Incest with a Parent." **Journal of the
American Academy of Child Psychiatry,** 5: 111-124, 1966.

A case of a thirteen year old boy who was incestuously
abused by his mother is presented. His mother is described
as having come from a very large family that was religiously
conservative. She had been raped at the age of twelve by
a brother-in-law and was severely punished by her parents
for her supposedly participant role in the rape. She married
young and was frequently separated from her husband who
was an alcoholic and was physically abusive. After their
divorce, she began drinking heavily and married two more
times. Diagnosed as having a hysterical personality disorder,
she had a tendency to sexualize all interpersonal relationships,
including the mother-son relationship. This is hypothesized
to be a product of her unconscious need to get revenge against
her parents for their punishment of her after the rape.

The Sons in Maternal Incest

Except for considerations as to whether the son initiated
the incest, little is known about the role that he may play
in the family prior to and during the incest. Considerably
more information is contained in the literature, however,
on the effects that maternal incest is likely to have on the
son, especially as he matures into adulthood.

265. de Young, M. **The Sexual Victimization of Children.**
Jefferson, N.C.: McFarland, 1982.

The same role reversal that occurs in cases of father-
daughter incest also occurred in the two cases of mother-son
incest in the sample. Both of the sons assumed a "little father"
role in the family, although the degree to which collusion
by the fathers encouraged this is unclear. The incest "affair"
is characterized by less coercion, distortion of reality and
morality, and less physical violence than is the case in father-
daughter incest, and it is hypothesized that those factors
may have contributed to the considerably fewer instances
of acting out and behavioral disturbances in the sons while
they were being victimized. Interviewed shortly after the
termination of the incest, both of the young sons were withdrawn, quiet, and very reticent to discuss their experiences.
Neither of the sons is mentally ill, nor does he demonstrate
sexual identity problems.

Incest Bibliography 96

266. Finch, S.M. "Adult Seduction of the Child: Effects on the Child." **Human Sexuality**, 7: 170-187, 1973.

A twelve year old boy, the victim of maternal incest, is described as effeminant in demeanor, unathletic, and as having openly demonstrated a preference for being a girl. The possible impact of maternal incest on the son's psychosexual development is discussed.

267. Meiselman, K.C. **Incest: A Psychological Study of Causes and Effects with Treatment Recommendations.** San Francisco: Jossey-Bass, 1978.

Two adult males who had been incestuously victimized by their mothers during their childhood and adolescence demonstrate significant mental health and behavioral problems. One engaged in delinquent acts as a youth, became an alcoholic as an adult, and despite a strong marriage and good relationship with his children, would frequently seek out prostitutes whom he would verbally humiliate and then refuse to pay. The second son is married and has children, a stable job, and occupational success. He is plagued with suicidal ideation, however, and obsessively thinks about incest while having sexual intercourse with his wife. Pedophilic fantasies are frightening and strongly defended against. On occasion he would cross-dress in his wife's clothes. Upon entering psychotherapy, he was diagnosed as a borderline psychotic. It is hypothesized that the most severe impact of maternal incest is on the son's psychosexual development and identity and that it is less likely to be a contributing factor to adult psychosis than some researchers have believed.

268. Nasjleti, M. "Suffering in Silence: The Male Incest Victim." **Child Welfare**, 49(5): 269-275, May 1980.

Nine male victims of paternal incest, ranging in age from twelve to seventeen, show a consistent pattern of extreme resistance to describing their molestation experiences in a group therapy setting. Clinging to the cultural concept of masculinity that emphasizes aggressiveness, non-dependence, non-nurturance, and physical strength, the boys who were molested by their mothers exhibit considerable shame for not having been the dominant person controlling the molestation experience. A review of the literature reveals that rapists, incest offenders, homosexuals and schizophrenics all report a high incidence of maternal incest in their backgrounds, suggesting that the most negative impact of this type of incest is on the psychosexual development of the son.

269. Yorukaglu, A. and Kemph, J.P. "Children Not Severely Damaged by Incest with a Parent." **Journal of the American Academy of Child Psychiatry,** 5: 111-124, 1966.

A case of a thirteen year old son who was incestuously abused by his mother is presented. Although the youngster did not develop a psychotic reaction to the incest, he showed marked behavioral disturbances characterized by fire setting, sexually inappropriate and aggressive behavior with other children, and had to be hospitalized in a psychiatric facility.

Brief Cases

Researchers' apparent fascination with mother-son incest has not produced a wealth of detailed observations and generalizable data. Unlike the references on father-daughter incest, the literature on the topic is primarily descriptive in nature, utilizing small samples and retrospective studies, and although many references on this topic are found in the professional literature, they generally lack the thorough analysis so often discovered in studies on other types of incest. A recent concern that emerges in the feminist literature on incest, in particular, is that in a patriarchal society the sexual victimization of boys is too often treated lightly, with perceptions that the boys enjoy the incest experience and benefit from it. Until that attitude is confronted and altered by researchers and theorists, the professional literature will not reflect the true nature of maternal incest and the impact it has on the sons.

The following references present brief case studies of mother-son incest.

270. Barry, M.J. and Johnson, A.M. "The Incest Barrier." **Psychoanalytic Quarterly,** 27: 485-500, 1958.

The case of a consensual, marriage-like relationship between a mother and son is described. Geographically isolated, the family had been abandoned by the alcoholic father when the son was twenty-three years old. Advised by the family physician to remain with his chronically ill mother and take his father's place in the family, the son apparently took that advice literally and developed a sexual relationship with his mother. Neither the mother nor the son was psychotic or mentally retarded.

271. Bender, L. and Blau, A. "The Reactions of Children to Sexual Relations with Adults." **American Journal of Orthopsychiatry,** 7: 500-518, 1937.

In this sample of sexually victimized children, there is one case of a six year old boy who was hospitalized after repeated attempts to have intercourse with his mother who allowed him to sleep with her. He had been separated from his mother the first four years of his life and began precociously acting out sexually after having been molested by his uncle. Behavior problems such as lying and stealing were noted, but the boy was not psychotic and did achieve a reasonable degree of adjustment during his adolescent years.

272. Berry, G.W. "Incest: Some Clinical Variations on a Classical Theme." **Journal of the American Academy of Psychoanalysis,** 3: 151-161, 1975.
The case of a seventeen year old young man is presented. He entered psychotheraphy because of anxiety related to homosexuality. He had been incestuously victimized by his mother.

273. Brown, W. "Murder Rooted in Incest." In **Patterns of Incest.** R.E.L. Masters (Ed.). New York: Julian Press, 1963.
An adopted adolescent son who seduced his widowed mother on several occasions is borderline mentally retarded and is a homosexual with a hair brush fetish. He murdered his mother when she discovered his collection of stolen brushes.

274. Kubo, S. "Researches and Studies on Incest in Japan." **Hiroshima Journal of Medical Sciences,** 8: 99-159, 1959.
A son, brain damaged by meningitis, was mentally retarded, violent and hypersexed. His widowed mother submitted to his sexual advances, believing that sexual release might deter him from repeated delinquency. After her death, he engaged in rape and exhibitionism, and later sexually assaulted his own daughters.

275. Lukianowicz, N. "Incest I: Paternal Incest; Incest II: Other Types of Incest." **British Journal of Psychiatry,** 120(556): 301-313, March 1972.
Three cases of mother-son incest are presented. One mother is described as a chronic schizophrenic who initiated incest with her retarded eleven year old son; the other mothers are portrayed as very dependent on their sons in the absence

of their husbands. One is neurotic and the other experienced depression created by guilt feelings about the incest. Two of the sons are schizophrenic.

276. Medlicott, R.W. "Parent-Child Incest." **Australia and New Zealand Journal of Psychiatry,** 1: 180-187, 1967.

The case of an adult male, apparently suffering from schizophrenia, is presented. As a child he had a sexual relationship with his mother at the command of auditory hallucinations. A second case of a man who as a child and adolescent had slept with his mother and then later became schizophrenic is also described.

277. Raphling, D.L.; Carpenter, B.L.; and Davis, A. "Incest: A Geneological Study." **Archives of General Psychiatry,** 16(4): 505-511, April 1967.

Incest victimization in three generations of a family is described to illustrate the social learning theory of incest. In one generation, the son witnessed intercourse between his father and sister; apparently stimulated by that, he sexually approached his sister as well. At the age of fourteen, his mother seduced him into fondling her genitals. This happened only on one occasion; frightened and confused by the incident, he refused to do it again despite her requests. As an adult he incestuously abused his three daughters and encouraged his son to make sexual advances to his mother. The man functioned well in his job and in the community, was not psychotic, but did display a paranoic defensive system and sadistic tendencies in sexual relationships.

278. Shelton, W.R. "A Study of Incest." **International Journal of Offender Therapy and Comparative Criminology,** 19: 139-153, 1975.

One of the cases in this court referred sample of four cases is that of a twenty-one year old man who experienced a psychotic episode after his father's death. He entered his mother's bedroom in the middle of the night and had sexual intercourse with her. Rationalizing that he was mentally disturbed, his mother did not resist.

279. Weinberg, S.K. **Incest Behavior.** New York: Citadel, 1955.

In this sample of 203 cases of reported incest, there are two cases of mother-son incest. In one of the cases, the adolescent son who had been separated from his mother for several years, raped her as an act of revenge for her abandonment. In the second case, a mentally retarded son was incestuously approached by his mother, a neurotic, lonely woman who had intercourse with him when he was twenty-eight years old.

Mother–Daughter Incest

There is no other type of nuclear family incest that has received less scrutiny than mother–daughter incest. The lack of studies in this area might suggest that the occurrence of these types of cases is so rare that creating a sample of any size is a difficult task. Since so many cases of incest are discovered in psychotherapy caseloads, the absence of mother–daughter cases may also hint that deleterious effects from this type of incest are infrequent. The following references deal with mother–daughter incest.

280. de Young, M. **The Sexual Victimization of Children.** Jefferson, N.C.: McFarland, 1982.
Two mothers who incestuously victimized their daughters are described. One of the women had been raised by her grandparents in severely economically deprived conditions. She had been raped by an uncle on two separate occasions. Married at sixteen, she had a daughter; after her husband left, she remarried and had five sons, and then created within the family a we-they split that left her sons to interact with her husband and her daughter to interact with her. After sexually withdrawing from her husband, she initiated a three year sexual relationship with her daughter. The second woman was born to fanatically religious and physically abusive parents who frequently punished her with sexual tortures. Pregnant at fifteen, she ran away from home and raised her daughter alone, developing an isolated and extremely symbiotic relationship with her. Because she identified so strongly with her daughter, she engaged in sex with her in order to give her the love she had been denied as a child. Their incestuous relationship lasted seven years. Neither of the daughters experienced any acting out or behavioral problems, although psychological problems related to depression began to develop after the incest was terminated by their mothers. It is hypothesized that the daughters may have experienced a delayed grief reaction to the loss of their dependent and emotionally satisfying relationships with their mothers who both withdrew emotionally from their daughters when they terminated the incest. Neither

of the daughters view her mother's behavior as victimizing
in nature; extremely dependent, they both experienced depression when forced by their mothers to assume responsible
and independent roles outside of the family.

281. Medlicott, R.W. "Parent-Child Incest." **Australia
and New Zealand Journal of Psychiatry,** 1: 180-187, 1967.
The case of a mother who initiated sexual play with
her daughter during her adolescence so that she did not
have to have a sexual relationship with her husband is described. The girl experienced chronic tension, frequent head-
aches, and significant sexual fears as an adolescent and
young adult.

282. Meiselman, K.C. **Incest: A Psychological Study
of Causes and Effects with Treatment Recommendations.**
San Francisco: Jossey-Bass, 1978.
One case of mother-daughter incest is presented. The
mother is described as extremely religious and suspicious
of people outside of the family. Developing a close, symbiotic
relationship with her daughter, she began conducting "pelvic
exams" on her when she suspected that her husband was
sexually molesting her. As a young adult, the daughter had
problems in forming satisfying relationships with men; she
was sexually promiscuous and experienced episodes of extreme
depression that motivated her to seek psychotherapy.

283. Weiner, I.B. "On Incest: A Survey." **Excerpta Criminology,** 4: 137-155, 1964.
The case of a daughter who had lived in foster homes
since infancy and who at the age of twenty-six was reunited
with her mother, is presented. The two had a consensual
lesbian relationship for a brief period of time. The daughter
was hospitalized for depression after the termination of
the affair.

8

Other Types of Incest

The professional literature contains only a few references to types of incest other than paternal, sibling, or maternal. The paucity of research in this area may reflect the relative rarity of these types of incest, or it may be taken as a suggestion that these types of incest do not produce effects deleterious enough to motivate victims to report or to enter into psychotherapy. An alternative explanation is that the degree of relatedness between the perpetrator and the victim in these cases, being at least once removed from the nuclear family, grants the family a certain amount of control over the future well being and the safety of the child. If parents can assure themselves that the incestuous uncle, as an example, is not allowed to visit, or that the incestuous grandfather, as another example, is never left alone with the children, they may be more inclined to treat the incest as a family matter that does not require the intervention of outside agencies. Cases such as these that are not reported would be unlikely to find their way into samples for study and therefore would show up infrequently in the professional literature.

Uncle–Niece Incest

Uncles play varying roles in the family system. Some have known the child victim since birth and have participated with a great degree of activity and emotional involvement in her life; in contrast, others are transitory figures, coming into the family system and the child's life only on rare occasions, only to leave again before strong emotional bonds have been created. And some uncles are surrogate fathers, their relationship to the child characterized by as intimate a tie as can be approximated by someone who is not the parent of the child.

The degree of relatedness, both by blood and by emotional intimacy, between the child and the perpetrator of the incest, is an important variable in determining the impact that incest will have on the victim. For some of the children in the samples in these studies, an incestuous experience with an uncle is tantamount to having been molested by a stranger; for others, it approximates that of being incestuously victimized by a father. Therefore, the impact of uncle-niece incest on the victim will vary, as the following studies suggest.

284. Browning, D.H. and Boatman, B. "Incest: Children at Risk." **American Journal of Psychiatry,** 134(1): 69-72, January 1977.

In a sample of fourteen victims of incest, three had been incestuously abused by an uncle, and two more had experienced incest victimization by a number of family members, including uncles. In all cases, the uncles are maternal uncles and none of the cases was reported because the family preferred to handle it on its own. Most of the victims in this sample appear to have an unusually dependent relationship on their mothers, yet often behave in a pseudomature, pseudoseductive fashion with others.

285. de Young, M. **The Sexual Victimization of Children.** Jefferson, N.C.: McFarland, 1982.

Three cases of uncle-niece incest are presented. All three of the uncles are maternal uncles who had been raised, themselves, in incestuous families. Although none was a victim of incest, each was a vicarious participant in the victimization of his sister, the child's mother. All three of the uncles have a significant emotional tie to their sisters' families, often assuming a surrogate father role. The nieces, all very young, are being raised in patriarchal homes in which adult authority, particularly male adult authority, is never questioned or challenged, and in which their passive, dependent mothers, who had been incestuously victimized themselves, could not play a protective role. All three of the nieces experienced psychosomatic complaints that may have been more related to their age at the time of the incest rather than their relationship to the offender. One of the nieces also developed a depressive reaction which significantly interfered with her school performance.

286. Finkelhor, D. **Sexually Victimized Children.** New York: The Free Press, 1979.

A survey with questions about childhood sexual experiences with adults and children, incestuous sexual experiences, and coercive sexual experiences at any age was administered to 796 New England college and university students. Of the 530 female respondents, sixteen report having been incestuously victimized by an uncle. When asked to rate the degree of emotional trauma experienced as a result of the incest on a scale from 1 to 5, with one representing a positive experience and five representing a negative experience, the mean trauma score for the respondents was 4.0.

287. Greenland, C. "Incest." **British Journal of Delinquency,** 9: 62–65, 1958.

The details of one case of uncle-niece incest are presented. The victim experienced extreme emotional trauma as a result of the incest and it is hypothesized that the negative impact was due to the fact that the uncle was a surrogate father to the niece.

288. Meiselman, K.C. **Incest: A Psychological Study of Causes and Effects with Treatment Recommendations.** San Francisco: Jossey-Bass, 1978.

Five cases of uncle-niece incest are found in this psychotherapy sample; two of those involved victimization by the father as well. It is hypothesized that the "typical" case of uncle-niece incest involves an uncle who is quite distant from his niece's nuclear family and plays no important role in her upbringing; consequently, the impact of the incest is comparatively less on the child. Uncle-niece incest has the potential of being extremely disturbing, however, if it is violent or if its occurrence disrupts the child's relationship with members of the nuclear family.

Uncle-Nephew Incest

There is only one reference in the professional literature on the dynamics of uncle-nephew incest.

289. Machota, P.; Pittman, F.S.; and Flomenhaft, K. "Incest as a Family Affair." **Family Process,** 6(1): 98–116, 1967.

A case of uncle-nephew incest occurring in two generations of a family is presented to illustrate the social learning model of incest. The nephew had been incestuously victimized by his uncle as a child, and many years later his own sons were victimized by the same uncle. The nephew denied for many years the reality of the abuse of his sons so that he did not have to confront his own experiences and the guilt and shame they created.

Grandfather–Granddaughter Incest

The popular stereotype of the "dirty old man" often precludes people from taking seriously sexual approaches to children by their grandfathers. Frequently dismissed as having an age-diminished sex drive that renders their incestuous approaches benign and even amusing, the grandfathers do not seem to provoke the ire created by so many other types of incest. The victims, too, are often not judged as having been harmed by the incest, an assessment that is not always supported by the literature.

290. de Young, M. **The Sexual Victimization of Children.** Jefferson, N.C.: McFarland, 1982.

Two cases of grandfather–granddaughter incest are presented. Both had incestuously abused their own daughters years before, and although each had been physically violent in those incidents of incest, neither was with his granddaughter. It is hypothesized that the diminishment of their patriarchal authority with their grandchildren because of their transitory interaction with the family forced them to surrender some of their brutality. The granddaughters both live in patriarchal families and do not question adult authority; their mothers are passive and dependent and unable to protect their children. The grandfathers, perceiving a replication of the dynamics of their own families, capitalized on the nature of this family system and abused their granddaughters. Neither of the children, both very young at the time of the incest, appeared to have experienced any significant emotional trauma, and it is suggested that the absence of outstanding symptomatology is due to the gentleness of the molestation, and their perceptions of the grandfathers as loving, benign and essentially asexual because of their advanced years.

291. Goodwin, J.; Cormier, L.; and Owen, J. "Grandfather–Granddaughter Incest: A Trigenerational View." **Child Abuse and Neglect,** 7(2): 163-170, 1983.

Demographics are given on ten incestuous grandfathers ranging in age from fifty to sixty-five years old. Most of the grandfathers had incestuously abused their own children and/or other children, and are therefore diagnosed as fixated

pedophiles. The eighteen granddaughters in the sample range
in age from one to eighteen years old. Only two are asympto-
matic, and it is hypothesized that the effects of grandfather
incest are most negative on the granddaughters who live
in chaotic, disorganized families; they experience severe
behavioral and educational symptoms related to the incest.
Those from more stable families are less negatively affected
and tend to demonstrate mild phobic reactions. Contrary
to popular belief, this type of incest is not at all benign.

292. Meiselman, K.C. **Incest: A Psychological Study
of Causes and Effects with Treatment Recommendations.**
San Francisco: Jossey-Bass, 1978.

In a psychotherapy sample there are five women who
report incest with their grandfathers; in two of the cases,
the women had also been abused by a father and an uncle,
respectively. None of the grandfathers was described as
senile, psychotic, mentally retarded, or alcoholic. All were
gentle in their sexual approaches and did not use threats
or other coercive tactics. The granddaughters all blamed
themselves for the incest, and all experienced problems
in later heterosexual relationships that they themselves
attributed to the incest.

Grandmother-Granddaughter Incest

There is only one brief reference in the professional
literature to the dynamics of grandmother-granddaughter
incest.

293. Barry, M.J. and Johnson, A.M. "The Incest Barrier."
Psychoanalytic Quarterly, 27: 485-500, 1958.

A case of a girl who had engaged in mutual genital
stimulation with her paternal grandmother when requested
by the chronically ill woman to share her bed, is described.
The girl terminated the relationship when she was fifteen,
later became a nurse, and entered psychotherapy because
of the disturbing hostile feelings she harbored towards elderly
female patients.

Other Types of Incest

Presumably other types of incest occur as well, but
references to them are not found in the literature. One

reference, however, which is a statistical study has data about the extent of incestuous victimization for a large sample and gives the mean trauma score the respondents estimated for the incest's impact on them as children and adolescents.

294. Finkelhor, D. **Sexually Victimized Children.** New York: The Free Press, 1979.

A survey with questions about childhood sexual experiences with adults and children, incestuous sexual experiences, and coercive sexual experiences at any age was administered to 796 New England college and university students who were also asked to rate the traumatic impact of the sexual abuse on them with a scale of 1 to 5, with one indicating a positive impact, and five indicating a negative impact. For male and female respondents who disclosed a history of incest victimization, the type of incest and the mean trauma scores are as follows:

Partner	Males ($\bar{x}$ tr. score)		Females ($\bar{x}$ tr. score)	
Uncle	1	(3.0)	16	(4.0)
Aunt	1	(no ans.)	0	
Grandfather	0		1	(4.0)
Cousin, male	9	(3.0)	48	(3.1)
Cousin, female	33	(2.4)	16	(2.4)
Brother-in-law	0		5	(4.0)

9

Systems Intervention in Incest

It is estimated that only a small percentage of incest cases are ever disclosed to any one or more of the societal systems set up to intervene in cases of reported incest. The characteristics of the abuser and the roles played by other family members create a secretive, enmeshed, and isolated family system that discourages both the disclosure of incest as well as outside inquiries into the nature of the family. When incest is disclosed or discovered, however, a chain of events, each more formalized and bureaucratized than the latter, is set into motion. What was once secret is now made increasingly more public; what was once all too real is now treated with skepticism; what was once private and personal is now under the control of others—these are some of the paradoxes encountered when the various systems garner their resources to intervene in cases of reported incest.

As well intentioned as each system is, none is flawless. At times the goals of one seem to be at odds with those of another, philosophies are not always consistent, errors in judgment are made, and victims and families sometimes fall into the cracks between systems. References in the literature often have been critical of systems intervention in cases of incest and have proposed reforms to make the system more fair and more responsive to the needs of the victims, perpetrators, and the incestuous families.

Disclosure of Incest

An adult's disclosure of a childhood history of incest many years after the fact may be treated skeptically, for whatever reason, by some people, but is more often than not believed. Those who are told may defensively distort, or minimize, or even exaggerate the nature of the incestuous abuse and its impact on the victim, but the account and

9

the aftermath are generally taken as a true rendering of a childhood event.

Much more skepticism attends the disclosure of incest by a child, however. That report that has the potential to mobilize the intervening systems and the power to break the secrecy of incest has created a great deal of controversy in the professional literature, as the following references indicate.

295. Ferenczi, S. "Confusion of Tongues Between Adults and the Child." **International Journal of Psychoanalysis,** 30: 225–230, 1949.

Because of overwhelming feelings of helplessness and anxiety, very young children who have been victimized by an adult will experience confusion about whether the event actually occurred and may deny the reality of it when confronted by an adult.

296. Freud, S. "The Aetiology of Hysteria." **The Complete Psychological Works of Sigmund Freud,** translated by J. Strachey, Standard Edition. London, England: Hogarth Press, 1962.

Women suffering from hysteria often report experiences of childhood sexual abuse, frequently with a family member. These reports are to be treated skeptically since they may represent a "defensive fiction" or fantasies created by the patients on the basis of their own unacceptable incestuous wishes.

297. Kaplan, S.L. and Kaplan, S.J. "The Child's Accusation of Sexual Abuse During a Divorce and Custody Struggle." **Hillside Journal of Clinical Psychiatry,** 3(1): 81–95, 1981.

Divorce and custody hearings bring out extremes in behavior. A case of two siblings who accused their father of incest during a custody battle is described in detail. Although it is unclear as to whether one of the siblings had actually been incestuously abused, the allegation of the second sibling who had not really been abused is explained in terms of a folie à deux, a transference of delusional material and/or abnormal behavior from one person to another who is in close association with the person affected primarily.

298. Masson, J.M. **The Assault on Truth: Freud's Suppression of the Seduction Theory.** New York: Farrar, Straus and Giroux, 1984.

Personal correspondence between Sigmund Freud and

Wilhelm Fliess reveal that Freud initially believed that paternal incest as well as other types of child sexual abuse were
the root causes of hysteria, but that he revised the theory
and relegated the allegations of sexual abuse to the fantasies
of his patients because of his own difficulty in accepting
the possibility that incest was so prevalent, and because
of his uncomfortable awareness of his own incestuous wishes
toward his daughter.

299. Peters, J.J. "Children Who Are Victims of Sexual
Assault and the Psychology of the Offender." **American
Journal of Psychotherapy**, 30(3): 398-421, July 1976.
Seven cases of children who have made allegations
of sexual abuse that were proven are presented and the
cultural and personal factors that cause professionals to
deny the reality of these disclosures are discussed in detail.
Relegating these traumas to the imagination of the children
tends to divert treatment from dealing with the source of
the problem, and although it may be a convenient assumption
for the therapist, it is counterproductive for the most efficient
resolution of the symptoms.

300. Rosenfeld, A.A.; Nadelson, C.C.; and Krieger,
M. "Incest and Sexual Abuse of Children." **Journal of the
American Academy of Child Psychiatry**, 16: 327-339, 1977.
When an actual traumatic incest event has occurred
in childhood, it may be repressed, displaced, or substituted
for a memory of a less traumatic event. Consequently, the
child's disclosure of the incest may be vague, inconsistent,
or casually delivered.

301. Rosenfeld, A.A.; Nadelson, C.C.; and Krieger,
M. "Fantasy and Reality in Patient Reports of Incest." **Journal
of Clinical Psychiatry**, 40(4): 159-164, April 1979.
The line of demarcation between fantasy and reality
is often hazy since the fantasy may be based upon real-life
family experiences that have been displaced or distorted.
Children over the age of nine who give a clear report of
sexual victimization should be believed since it is at that
age that a child is able to clearly differentiate between
fantasy and reality; before that age, in the absence of corroborating evidence, reports should be treated skeptically. Therapists dealing with clients of any age who report sexual abuse
should consider whether the disclosure could be an incorrectly reported fantasy from childhood; whether the family of the person was overstimulating; whether actual mo-

lestation has occurred but the wrong person is being accused; whether the person making the report is psychiatrically disturbed; whether there is an ulterior motive for making a false allegation; and whether there are extenuating circumstances such as divorce or custody battle that may motivate the leveling of false charges.

302. Rush, F. "Freud and the Sexual Abuse of Children." **Chrysalis**, 1: 31-45, 1977.
The author discusses the reasons behind Freud's suppression of the seduction theory and his contention that children fantasize and incorrectly report allegations of incest.

Professionals' Responsibility Upon Disclosure or Discovery

Once incest has been disclosed or discovered, professional people who may intei ct with the victim and his or her family in any one of a variety of different capacities now may play a significant role. The following references deal with the issues of the necessity of reporting incest and the barriers to that reporting that many hesitant or skeptical professional people create for themselves.

303. Burgess, A.W.; Holmstrom, L.L.; and McCausland, M.P. "Child Sexual Assault by a Family Member: Decisions Following Disclosure." **Victimology: An International Journal,** 2(2): 236-250, Summer 1977.
Forty-four youngsters between the ages of eighteen months and sixteen years who had been incestuously victimized were treated at a pediatric walk-in clinic of a metropolitan hospital. Incest victimization can be discovered in one or more of the following ways: through physical and behavioral clues demonstrated by the child; through the accounts of witnesses to the abuse; and through the allegations made by the child. Divided loyalties within incestuous families interfere with decisions after disclosure, as these cases demonstrate. Many of the families in the sample preferred to handle the abuse as a private family matter and were willing to voluntarily enter psychotherapy. Mandatory reporting laws for medical professionals require that cases of incest be reported regardless of the family's intentions.

304. Denham, P.L. "Toward an Understanding of Child Rape." **Journal of Pastoral Care,** 36(4): 235-245, 1982.
The hospital chaplain's responsibilities in cases of

child sexual abuse are discussed. As a minister whose expertise is in the area of family and individual functioning, the chaplain is a guide and an educator and must serve as an advocate for the child and the family with the hospital staff and with the police.

305. James, J.; Womack, W.M.; and Strauss, F. "Physician Reporting of Sexual Abuse of Children." **Journal of the American Medical Association,** 240(11): 1145-1146, September 1978.

A random sample of six hundred pediatricians and general practitioners in Seattle, Washington was sent a questionnaire eliciting information regarding their frequency of contact with sexually abused children, the types of sexual abuse encountered in their practice, their procedure for reporting, and the treatment or referral for treatment provided. Replies tabulated for the ninety-six returned surveys indicate that over half of the respondents saw at least one sexually abused child a year in their practice, and treated from one to seven suspected cases each year. Over one-half of these children are judged by the physicians to have been seriously to very seriously traumatized by the abuse, yet only 42% of the physicians reply that they would report any case of child sexual abuse, despite a mandatory reporting law in that state. The reluctance to report reflects the respondents' dissatisfaction with social service agency intervention in these cases, and their opinion that such intervention actually would be more harmful than beneficial to the child and his or her family.

306. Riggs, R.S. "Incest: The School's Role." **Journal of School Health,** 52(6): 365-370, August 1982.

A reluctance to go home after school, frequent absences from school that are justified by the father or the male guardian, the reticence of the child to undress for physical education classes, and seductive behavior on the part of the child are all indicators of incest. All suspected cases should be reported immediately and the school system should offer supportive counseling for the child once the disclosure of the incest has been made. Parent-teacher education on incest is stressed as is education on the topic for children in a classroom setting.

Intervention

Once incest is disclosed or discovered, the first systems to intervene are usually the police and/or the protective services department. Seeing the child and the family shortly after disclosure and eliciting information that is needed to protect the child from further abuse, assess the family's prognosis for therapy, and prepare evidence for the possible criminal prosecution of the perpetrator, requires finely honed interviewing and investigation skills, both of which are discussed in the following references.

307. Burgess, A.W. and Holmstrom, L.L. "Interviewing Young Victims." In **Sexual Assault of Children and Adolescents;** A.W. Burgess, A.N. Groth, L.L. Holmstrom and S.M. Sgroi, Lexington, Massachusets: Lexington Books, 1978.

Three factors need to be assessed when interviewing a child victim of sexual assault: who reported the assault; what is the timing of the assault in relationship to the interview; and what is the emotional reaction of the child to the assault. The interviewer must establish trust with the child by creating a gently supportive environment and by using the child's language during the interview. Details about the assault must be ascertained and the child's emotional reaction to it must be assessed. The use of age-related media, such as toys, dolls, and art supplies, may help the child express both the details of the sexual assault and his or her feelings about it.

308. Flamming, C.J. "Interviewing Child Victims of Sex Offenders." **Police,** 16(6): 23-28, 1972.

Interviewing is based upon different objectives than interrogation; it is a purposeful communication technique designed to seek information once rapport has been established. Police officers must develop this skill for interviewing child victims of sexual assault. The interview should be conducted in a place that feels safe to the child and which guarantees some privacy; male officers should not interview female victims without someone else present as a witness. In order to assess the child's capability of being a witness in the event the case is taken to court, the police officer must not only gather information about the nature of the offense, but must also determine the victim's maturity level, concept of time, and general truthfulness.

309. Keefe, M.L. "Police Investigation in Child Sexual

Assault." In **Sexual Assault of Children and Adolescents;**
A.W. Burgess, A.N. Groth, L.L. Holmstrom, and S.M. Sgroi.
Lexington, Massachusetts: Lexington Books, 1978.

The initial function of the police officer is to establish
rapport with the victim by using language the child can
understand, and by allowing the child to tell the story in
his or her own words and at a comfortable pace. Coordination
with the protective services unit, the hospital, and the prosecuting attorney's office is also a necessary part of the police
officer's responsibility.

310. McCarty, L.M. "Investigation of Incest: Opportunity
to Motivate Families to Seek Help." **Child Welfare,** 60(10):
679-689, December 1981.

A model of the investigation of incest reports is presented and techniques for assuring the child is protected from
further abuse and the families are motivated for treatment
are discussed.

Medical Evaluation

Most cases of reported incest will require that the
child be examined medically for physical indicators of sexual
abuse. This examination must not only be thorough, it must
also be sensitive to the emotional condition of the victimized
child.

311. Burgess, A.W. and Laszlo, A.T. "Courtroom Use
of Hospital Records in Sexual Assault Cases." **The Sexual
Victimology of Youth;** L.G. Schultz (Ed.). Springfield, Illinois:
Charles C. Thomas, Publisher, 1980.

Based upon the counseling of over five hundred victims
of sexual assault treated at a large, metropolitan hospital,
the importance of care and precision in writing hospital
records is emphasized. Physical evidence accumulated during
the medical examination must be promptly and carefully
collected. Whenever possible, photographs should be taken
of the victim. Semen specimens are obtained by using a
swab and the examiner must note the quantity of the sperm
and the presence or absence of motility. Testing the vaginal
pool specimen for acid phosphates may be useful in indicating
the time interval since the assault. Evidence of tears, stains,
or soil marks on the victim's clothing may indicate a struggle
with the perpetrator, as do broken fingernails and skin scrap-
ings taken from under the nails. Loose hairs that cling to

the patient's body or clothing may also be used as evidence. A verbatim account by the patient should be included in the hospital record, and a precise descriptio: of signs of emotional trauma should also be included.

312. Sgroi, S.M. "Comprehensive Examination for Child Sexual Assault: Diagnostic, Therapeutic and Child Protection Issues." In **Sexual Assault of Children and Adolescents;** A.W. Burgess, A.N. Groth, L.L. Holmstrom, anć   ´1. Sgroi. Lexington, Massachusetts: Lexington Books, 1978.

The following information, if present upon medical examination, may be used as evidence of child sexual abuse: sperm recovered from the vagina or genital/rectal region of the female child; pregnancy; genital or rectal trauma in children of both sexes; gonorrhea infection; foreign bodies in the vagina of the female child or in the urethra or rectum of children of both sexes; statement of sexual assault by the treated child; corroborating statements of sexual assault by others; confession by the perpetrator; other physical evidence of trauma that supports the child's statement; and supporting material evidence such as blood or semen stains on the clothing.

313. Sgroi, S.M. "Kids With Clap: Gonorrhea as an Indicator of Child Sexual Assault." **Victimology: An International Journal,** 2(2): 251-267, Summer 1977.

Gonorrhea infections in children in any body site except for the eyes is a tell-tale indicator of child sexual abuse. The examination of the child in cases where sexual abuse is suspected should include a complete physical and developmental exam; skeletal x-rays for children under six years old; a genital exam with a vaginal smear; cultures of the throat, urethra, rectum and vagina, as well as blood tests to screen for venereal diseases.

The Child Incest Victim in Court

Comparatively few cases of incest are tried in a court of law. When they are, however, the child victims are frequently called upon as witnesses. Required to testify in the presence of strangers, family members, and the perpetrator of the abuse, a criminal trial inevitably is a stressful experience for the child. The careful preparation of the victim for the experience can do a great deal to reduce the "legal process trauma" that the insensitive handling

of these cases may produce. The literature has some references which deal with the preparation of children for testifying
in court in cases of incest.

314. Burgess, A.W. and Holmstrom, L.L. "The Child
and the Family During the Court Process." In **Sexual Assault
of Children and Adolescents;** A.W. Burgess, A.N. Groth,
L.L. Holmstrom, and S.M. Sgroi. Lexington, Massachusetts:
Lexington Books, 1978.

The court process for the child and family can be as
much of a crisis as the sexual assault. Victims are forced
to relive the assault and are confronted by people who are
skeptical of their account. For the prosecuting attorney,
a humanistic style is suggested with sensitivity to the socio-
emotional aspect of the process in which the child is involved.
Expert testimony may need to be included and the attorney
must develop a good working relationship with the expert.
In the courtroom, special attention should be paid to the
behavior of the child in order to assess his or her level of
stress. Tasks of professionals who orchestrate criminal
proceedings in cases of incest include neutralizing the family's
reactions to the courtroom process, supporting the child,
and dealing with the feelings of the child. For children and
adolescents, factors that decrease stress in the court are:
talking about the court process, visiting a courtroom before
the trial begins, having a parent or supportive adult present
during the trial, the use of clear and simple language when
questioning the youngster, and preparing the child for the
questions that might be asked by the defense attorney.

315. Stevens, D. and Berliner, L. "Special Techniques
for Child Witnesses." In **The Sexual Victimology of Youth;**
L.G. Schultz (Ed.). Springfield, Illinois: Charles C. Thomas,
Publisher, 1980.

Knowledge of the basic principles of child development
is necessary for police and prosecutors. The credibility of
the child as a witness must be established in the courtroom
by assessing the developmental level of the child. The family
or other supportive adults should be included throughout
the criminal justice process. Massive reforms in this process
are urged in order to protect already victimized children
from further trauma.

Legal Reforms

Because the criminal justice system can have such a negative impact on the child or adolescent incest victim when he or she is required to testify in a court of law, legal reforms have been urged in the professional literature.

316. Labai, D. "The Protection of the Child Victim of a Sexual Offense in the Criminal Justice System." **Wayne Law Review,** 15: 927-1032, 1969.

The degree of psychic trauma to the child victim of a sexual offense is very dependent upon the way he or she is treated after the disclosure or the discovery of the incest. "Legal process trauma" can be generated by the insensitive handling of these cases. The appointment and training of special police officers to deal with child victims can serve three cardinal purposes: the protection of the child's welfare; the guarantee of better methods of recording the child's statements; and the contribution to the quality and trustworthiness of police reports in court. All elements of the system need to be responsive to the needs of the victimized child. Several innovative models based on the procedures used in Israel and Denmark in cases of child sexual abuse are described in detail.

317. Ordway, D.P. "Parent-Child Incest: Proof at Trial Without Testimony in Court by the Victim." **Journal of Law Reform,** 150(1): 131-152, Fall 1981.

The incest victim should not have to personally testify in trial. Testimony should be replaced with tape-recorded pre-trial examinations of the victim by an expert who is trained in child psychology and the dynamics of incest. Strategies for doing that efficiently and without infringing on the defendant's constitutional rights are discussed.

318. Ordway, D.P. "Reforming Judicial Procedure for Handling Parent-Child Incest." **Child Welfare,** 62(1): 69-75, January/February 1983.

Current procedures for handling cases of incest in the criminal justice system have three shortcomings: they are harmful to the victim; they fail to take into account the complicated family dynamics in incestuous families; and they produce evidence that is not reliable in court. It is proposed that the child victim be interviewed by a trained expert who can handle the case and present the evidence in court so that the child does not have to personally testify.

Strategies for doing that effectively and without compromising
the constitutional rights of the defendant are discussed
in detail.

Other Types of Intervention

The incestuous abuse of children mobilizes a number
of different systems into action. Even if the case never
comes to a criminal trial, social services, mental health
and foster care systems may intervene in the lives of victimized children and their families. Some references in the
literature examine the functions and the problems with
the intervention of these systems into cases of reported
incest.

319. Adams, P.L. and Roddey, G.J. "Language Patterns
of Opponents to a Child Protection Program." **Child Psychiatry
and Human Development,** 11(3): 135-157, Spring 1981.
Incest creates strong feelings of disgust, revulsion,
disbelief, and even fascination in the professional people
who may develop a special vocabulary that functions to
deny the reality of incest and to obscure the effects it has
on victims.

320. Finkelhor, D. "Removing the Child—Prosecuting
the Offender in Cases of Sexual Abuse: Evidence from the
National Reporting System for Child Abuse and Neglect."
Child Abuse and Neglect, 7(2): 195-205, 1983.
Data analyzed on 6,096 reported cases of child sexual
abuse in 1978 reveal that foster placement occurred in more
cases of child sexual abuse than in cases of the physical
abuse of children. The children who are the most likely to
be placed in foster care are older incest victims who had
reported their own victimization. Criminal action is taken
five times more often in sexual abuse cases than physical
abuse cases, and most often in cases directly reported to
the police, and in cases in which the perpetrator of the sexual
abuse has a criminal record. Analysis of data demonstrates
that race and socioeconomic conditions of the families are
not variables in decision-making.

321. Furniss, T. "Mutual Influence and Interlocking
Professional-Family Process in the Treatment of Child Sexual
Abuse and Incest." **Child Abuse and Neglect,** 7(2): 207-223,
1983.

Three types of intervention, police, social service, and therapeutic, are described and the effects that each has on the family and the victim of child sexual abuse are discussed. Techniques by which individual family members may attempt to manipulate a system or play one system off against another are also described. Finally, a model for the interlocking of the systems in order to serve families and victimized children is proposed.

10

Treatment of Incest Victims
and Families

Therapeutic intervention with incest victims and with
incestuous families only recently has been recognized as
an area of specialty. Although the modalities vary widely,
each treatment approach is predicated upon the assumptions
that incest often has deleterious short- and longterm effects
for the victim, and that incestuous families are by nature
pathological.

One treatment approach stressed in the literature
focuses on the individual incest victim. The following references examine this therapeutic modality, discuss presenting
symptoms, identify problem areas, and offer caveats to
the therapists who treat clients with a history of incest
victimization.

322. Cohen, J.A. "Theories of Narcissism and Trauma."
American Journal of Psychotherapy, 35(1): 93–100, January
1981.

Clinical material is presented to illustrate that incest
is experienced as a traumatic event by the victim and that
it interferes with the formation and registration of normal
memory traces and wishes. The repetition of this trauma
over time creates a narcissistic defensive structure which
causes special problems with transference during therapy.
Utilizing a psychoanalytic approach, the author proposes
a treatment model of structural change that assists the
ego in undoing the damage it has done to itself.

323. Courtois, C.E. and Watts, D.L. "Counseling Adult
Women Who Experienced Incest in Childhood or Adolescence."
Personnel and Guidance Journal, 60(5): 275–297, January
1982.

Incest is defined as sexual contact with a person who
would be considered an ineligible partner because of blood

and/or social ties to the subject and her family. The incest victim enters therapy with problems in self-esteem and in her relationship with others. The facilitation of emotional catharsis, the confrontation and assimilation of feelings, the creation of a positive self-concept and the healthy management of life's tasks are the goals of therapy. Incest must be viewed as sexual assault by therapists who must be cognizant of their own personal feelings about incest as well as the biases that may have been created by training and education within certain theoretical frameworks. Difficulties in validating the victims' experiences because of an overidentification with the father may occur for male therapists; female therapists, in turn, may overidentify with the victim. Therapeutic progress is likely to be slow and will test the patience and timing of the therapist.

324. de Young, M. "Case Reports: The Sexual Exploitation of Incest Victims by Helping Professionals." **Victimology: An International Journal**, 6(1–4): 92–100, 1981.

Therapeutic techniques for victimizing the incest victim, including not believing disclosures of incest, failing to report or to intervene in on-going incest victimization, and blaming the victim are discussed. Three cases of adult women who had been sexually exploited by their therapists after disclosing a history of incest are presented, as well as one case of a psychologist who had entered into a sexual relationship with one of his clients who had a history of incest victimization.

325. Giaretto, H. **Integrated Treatment of Child Sexual Abuse.** Palo Alto, California: Science and Behavior Books, 1982.

Treatment and training models from the Child Sexual Abuse Treatment Program of Santa Clara County, California are presented in detail.

326. Krieger, M.J.; Rosenfeld, A.A.; Gordon, A.; and Bennett, M. "Problems in the Psychotherapy of Children with Histories of Incest." **American Journal of Psychotherapy**, 34(1): 81–88, January 1980.

Seventy-three court-referred incestuously victimized girls are "participant victims" in that they had encouraged the initiation and continuation of the incest. Each had behaved seductively towards the therapist because of her identification with the aggressor, the reinforcement she had received at home for this behavior, and her need to control the emotional intimacy that occurs within the therapeutic relationship.

327. McCarthy, B. "Incest and Psychotherapy." **Irish Journal of Psychotherapy,** 1: 11-16, September 1982.
The Freudian theory of incest is analyzed and three cases of incest victims treated with a psychoanalytic model are presented.

328. Mayer, A. **Incest: A Treatment Manual for Therapy with Incest Victims, Spouses and Offenders.** Holmes Beach, Florida: Learning Publications, Inc., 1983.
This is a manual for therapists which describes the treatment models and techniques for working with incest victims, offenders, and with incestuous families.

329. Slager-Jorne', P. "Counseling Sexually Abused Children." **Personnel and Guidance Journal,** 57(2): 103-105, October 1978.
Sexual abuse is defined as exposing a child to sexual stimulation inappropriate for the child's age, level of psychosexual development, and role in the family. Five cases of sexually abused children referred to therapy are presented. Each experienced anxiety which created phobias, tics, nightmares, enuresis, eating disorders and sexual acting out. Therapists are encouraged to create a supportive, understanding environment in which the presenting symptoms are treated until the child is able and willing to discuss the sexual abuse.

330. Westerlund, E. "Counseling Women with Histories of Incest." **Women and Therapy,** 2(4): 17-31, Winter 1982.
Incest is defined as any form of sexual abuse that takes place between an adult and a child or between an older child and a younger child within the same family. Women with histories of incest enter therapy with problems in self-esteem, feelings of guilt, sexual dysfunction, and a range of self-defeating behaviors. Therapists are encouraged to be aware of their own sexual attitudes, and to give their clients control by utilizing a nondirective, nonsexist approach that defines and respects boundaries.

Family Therapy

Family therapy is another well documented approach to the treatment of incest. This modality assumes that incest is a product of family dysfunction and that to create a safe and healthy environment for the child, the entire family must be treated. The following references focus on the family therapy model.

331. Anderson, L.M. and Shafer, G. "The Character-Disordered Family: A Community Treatment Model for Family Sexual Abuse." **American Journal of Orthopsychiatry,** 49(3): 436-445, July 1979.

An analogy is made between the sociopathic character disorder and the paternally incestuous family. On the basis of the examination of sixty-two paternally incestuous families referred for treatment, it is proposed that the families have characteristics similar to that of the sociopath: they have marked deficits in impulse control and judgment; an impaired sense of responsibility; a history of conflictual relationships with authority figures; an inability to tolerate intimate relationships; narcissism; manipulativeness; dependency conflicts; and they experience little guilt and anxiety. Treatment success with these character-disordered families is measured not only by the cessation of the incest, but also by the development of egalitarian family interactions.

332. Barnard, C.P. (Editor). **Families, Incest and Therapy,** New York: Human Sciences Press, 1984.

A blend of theory, pragmatic considerations, and case illustrations is presented in this book which emphasizes treatment techniques and modalities for incestuous families.

333. Eist, H.I. and Mandel, A.U. "Family Treatment of Ongoing Incest Behavior." **Family Process,** 7(2): 216-232, September 1968.

The treatment approach taken with one incestuous family is described. Each member was treated individually before family therapy was initiated. The goals of therapy were the development of individual self-respect and honesty.

334. McCarty, L.M. "Investigation of Incest: Opportunity to Motivate Families to Seek Help." **Child Welfare,** 60(10): 679-689, December 1981.

A model of the investigation of incest reports is presented and techniques for assuring the child is protected from further abuse and the families are motivated for treatment are discussed.

335. Sagutun, I.J. "The Effects of Court-Ordered Therapy on Incest Offenders." **Journal of Offender Counseling, Services and Rehabilitation,** 5(3/4): 99-105, Spring/Summer 1981.

A self-report questionnaire was administered to ninety-two incestuous families to assess the level of responsibility for the incest and the changes in attitude that occurred as a result of therapy. Significant changes in a positive direction are measured for each area and were particularly noted for those families who were ordered to attend therapy by the court.

336. Sagutun, I.J. "Attributional Effects of Therapy with Incestuous Families." **Journal of Marital and Family Therapy**, 8(1): 99-104, January 1982.

Fifty-six male incest offenders and thirty-five spouses who are participants in a Parents United program in Los Angeles County, California completed a questionnaire that examined their attitudes about the cause of the incest, who is to blame, and their own role in it. Therapy significantly changed the attitudes of most of the offenders who began to assume responsibility for the incest. Although the therapy was not successful in keeping the families intact, it did significantly reduce the recidivism of the offenders.

337. Server, J.C. and Janzen, C. "Contraindications to Reconstitution of Sexually Abusive Families." **Child Welfare**, 61(5): 279-288, May 1982.

Many treatment programs emphasize family reconstitution as a goal, but in an analysis of forty-eight incestuous families referred to the Sexual Abuse Treatment Program in Baltimore, Maryland, rigid criteria for reconstitution are urged. The father must acknowledge responsibility for the incest; the therapist and all the family members must express reasonable assurance that the child is safe from further abuse; the daughter must express and demonstrate an ability to seek professional help in the event she is once again sexually approached; the mother must demonstrate a greater ability to protect her children and herself from abuse; sufficient progress must be made towards attaining treatment goals; the mother and daughter relationship must significantly improve; and generational boundaries must be strengthened before families are reunited.

338. Sgroi, S.M. "Family Treatment of Child Sexual Abuse." **Journal of Social Work and Human Sexuality**, 1(1-2): 109-128, Fall/Winter 1982.

Incestuous families must be considered as character-disordered and as generally resistive to treatment. Therapeutic goals with these families should include the creation of at least one adult ally for the victim within the family; an enhancement of communication patterns; the setting of limits within the family; the creation of clear and strong generational boundaries; and the decrease of social isolation.

339. Taubman, S. "Incest in Context." **Social Work,** 29(1): 35-40, January/February 1984.

An ecosystem approach to therapy is proposed in which family treatment occurs with special attention also given to the broader social and cultural attitudes and values that are conducive to sexual abuse and which may have impacted on the incestuous family.

340. Topper, A.B. "Options for Big Brother's Involvement in Incest." **Child Abuse and Neglect,** 3(1): 291-296, 1979.

Comparing a group of adult female incest victims to a group of adolescent female incest victims, the author concludes that therapeutic intervention must be swift, decisive, and directed towards the whole family.

Specialized Approaches

Specialized therapeutic approaches to incest victims and offenders are also documented in the literature. These include art therapy, marriage counseling, behavior modification and group therapy.

341. Carozza, P.M. and Heirsteiner, C.L. "Young Female Incest Victims in Treatment: Stages of Growth Seen With a Group Art Therapy Model." **Clinical Social Work Journal,** 10(3): 165-175, Fall 1982.

Significant changes in the drawings of incest victims occurred during their participation in art therapy which was carried out in a group context. Concomitant changes in self-esteem and in the behaviors of the victims are also documented.

342. Edwards, N.B. "Case Conference: Assertive Training in a Case of Homosexual Pedophilia." **Journal of Behavior Therapy and Experimental Psychiatry,** 3: 55-63, 1972.

Assertiveness training and thought-stopping techniques bring about significant positive changes in the behavior of a father who had incestuously abused his three sons.

343. Goodwin, J. "Use of Drawings in Evaluating Children Who May Be Incest Victims." **Children and Youth Services Review,** 4(3): 269-279, 1982.

Drawings can be used with the child victims to obtain more information about the offense and to respond to the child's need to escape from the traumatic situation into fantasy and play. The responses of nineteen female incest victims to a variety of structured and unstructured art therapy models are explained with the victims' drawings used to illustrate the responses.

344. Gordy, P.L. "Group Work That Supports Adult Victims of Childhood Incest." **Social Casework,** 64(5): 300-307, May 1983.

A time-limited group therapy approach for incest victims is described. The group focuses on topics for discussion that have particular relevance for victimized women: guilt feelings, mistrust of men, sexual dysfunction, and depression.

345. Harbert, T.L.; Barlow, D.H.; Hersen, M.; and Austin, J.B. "Measurement and Modification of Incestuous Behavior: A Case Study." **Psychological Reports,** 34: 79-86, 1974.

Covert sensitization is used to eliminate incestuous behavior in the case of a fifty-two year old man.

346. Knittle, B.J. and Tuana, S.J. "Group Therapy as Primary Treatment for Adolescent Victims of Intrafamilial Sexual Abuse." **Clinical Social Work Journal,** 8(4): 236-242, Winter 1980.

Incest victimization creates isolation, alienation, feelings of helplessness, distrust, guilt, shame, and self-defeating and self-destructive behaviors. A group therapy model is particularly helpful in resolving these problems for adolescent victims of incest.

347. Levin, S.M.; Barry, S.M.; Gambaro, S.; Wolfinsohn, L.; and Smith, A. "Variations in Covert Sensitization in the Treatment of Pedophilic Behavior: A Case Study." **Journal of Consulting and Clinical Psychology,** 45: 896-907, 1977.

Variations of covert sensitization are paired with aversion relief to eliminate the deviant sexual behavior of a thirty-nine year old incestuous male.

348. Siegel, J. "Intrafamilial Child Sexual Victimization: A Role Training Model." **Journal of Psychotherapy, Psychodrama and Sociometry,** 34(1): 37-43, 1981.

A role training model aimed at explaining and understanding the dynamics of incest and the availability of effective and appropriate responses to family crisis situations
is described.

349. Taylor, R.L. "Marital Therapy in the Treatment
of Incest." **Social Casework,** 65(4): 195-202, April 1984.

Understanding the marital dyad is crucial to the treatment of incest. Before marital therapy is undertaken, however,
the couple needs to agree that the offender is responsible
for the incest and that it is a harmful act; that the offender
needs to have a period of separation from the family; and
the mother needs to form an emotional bond with her daughter.

350. Tsai, M. and Wagner, N.N. "Therapy Groups for
Women Sexually Molested as Children." **Archives of Sexual
Behavior,** 7(5): 417-427, September 1978.

A group therapy model that stresses the expression
of feelings and the resolution of such incest-related issues
as guilt, depression, sexual dysfunctions and repetition compulsion is described.

Programs

Over the years a variety of innovative programs have
been developed for the treatment of incest. The following
references describe specific programs or deal with the larger
issue of program development and evaluation.

351. Bander, K.; Fein, E.; and Bishop, G. "Child Sexual
Abuse Treatment: Some Barriers to Program Operations."
Child Abuse and Neglect, 6(2): 185-191, 1982.

The Sexual Trauma Treatment Program in Hartford,
Connecticut is described and the demographics and the treatment concerns of the eighty-two incestuous families treated
there are discussed. Since these are multiproblem families,
the coordination of services is critical and barriers to that
are explained.

352. Giaretto, H. "A Comprehensive Child Sexual Abuse
Treatment Program." **Child Abuse and Neglect,** 6(3): 263-278,
1982.

The Child Sexual Abuse Treatment Program of Santa

Clara County, California is described and data on the more than 4,000 families treated there are presented.

353. Kroth, J.A. **Child Sexual Abuse.** Springfield, Illinois: Charles C. Thomas, Publisher, 1979.

This is a thorough empirical analysis of the Child Sexual Abuse Treatment Program of Santa Clara County, California, with special emphasis on the programs, treatment goals, training models and the computerized data system.

354. MacFarlane, K. and Bulkley, J. "Treating Child Sexual Abuse: An Overview of Current Program Models." **Journal of Social Work and Human Sexuality,** 1(1-2): 69-91, Fall/Winter 1982.

In 1981 there were over five hundred treatment centers across the country that specialized in child sexual abuse. Program models, philosophies and treatment strategies of the various types of agencies are described.

355. Paulson, M. "Incest and Sexual Molestation: Clinical and Legal Issues." **Journal of Clinical Child Psychology,** 7(3): 177-180, Fall 1978.

The UCLA Child Trauma Intervention Project, a multicultural, bilingual program for the diagnosis and treatment of incest and nonincestuous child molestation is described.

356. Wolvert, R.W.; Barron, N. and M.B. "Parents United of Oregon: A Natural History of a Self-Help Group for Sexually Abusive Families." **Prevention in Human Services,** 1(3): 99-109, Spring 1982.

A self-help group for incest offenders and their spouses is described and the evolution of the group from its conception through its achievement of its group goals is explained.

357. Zefran, J.; Riley, H.F.; Andersen, W.O.; Curtis, J.H.; Jackson, L.M.; Kelly, P.H.; McGury, E.T.; and Suriano, M.K. "Management and Treatment of Child Sexual Abuse Cases in a Juvenile Court Setting." **Journal of Social Work and Human Sexuality,** 1(1-2): 155-170, Fall/Winter 1982.

Fifty-five incestuous families were referred to the Special Services Unit for the Treatment of Child Sexual Abuse of the Cook County (Illinois) Juvenile Court. The characteristics of the incestuous families are described and the treatment and case management techniques for dealing with them are presented.

Review

Treatment strategies for work with incest victims, offenders and families are complex and involve a variety of modalities. The following article reviews the strategies as they are discussed in the literature.

358. Dixen, J. and Jenkins, J.O. "Incestuous Child Sexual Abuse: A Review of Treatment Strategies." **Clinical Psychology Review,** 1: 211-222, 1981.

A review of the literature shows that family therapy is most effective after the individual family members have been treated; insight-oriented therapy is the only therapy used for treatment of the longterm effects of incest for the victim; and a multicomponent treatment package for the abuser and the victim, as well as combinations of interventions, are especially effective as treatment strategies. This review of the literature contains fifty-six entries.

11

Statistical Studies

Social scientists, free from the psychoanalytic tradition that relegates accounts of incest to the fertile imaginings of the victims, were the first to accumulate data on child sexual abuse from large samples of subjects. More willing to accept disclosures of early sexual experiences as fact, the studies by these social scientists provide a wealth of information as to the nature of childhood sexual experiences and the impact these experiences have on the victims. The data are remarkably consistent as well: one-fifth to one-third of all women report childhood sexual encounters with an adult male; up to one-quarter of all women report experiences with a relative, the figure varying according to the definition of incest used in the study; and one woman in a hundred discloses an incestuous experience with her father or step-father. Similar data on the sexual abuse of males are less often reported in these studies, suggesting that although the psychoanalytic tradition in the interpretation of females' sexually abusive experiences has been circumvented, the rampant homophobia that denies the reality of the sexual abuse of males has not.

These statistical studies defy the popularly held belief that child sexual abuse in general, and incest in particular, are extremely rare phenomena. They also challenge the notion that such childhood sexual experiences are benign, neutral, or positive, as some researchers have insisted they are. In each of the studies that also ask the respondents to rate the psychological impact of the experience on them, the majority respond that they are largely negative experiences, and the data clearly demonstrate that as the degree of relatedness between the perpetrator of the sexual abuse and the victim becomes closer, the sexual encounters are perceived by the victim as much more damaging and disturbing.

Despite the data from these studies, there is every reason to believe that both the rate of childhood sexual abuse in general and of incest in particular is considerably higher than what these references demonstrate. The respondents in these studies invariably are white, middle class, educated individuals, and do not by color, class or intelligence represent the composition of the larger society. Their experiences, therefore, may differ in quantity and quality from those of other segments of the population.

In addition to the similarities in rates of occurrence and degrees of harmfulness found in these studies, other trends are also evident, and each suggests a prevention strategy. First, the vast majority of adults who perpetrate acts of child sexual abuse are males. The nature of the sex role stereotypes and the cultural expectations that create and encourage such sexually abusive behavior in males require thorough analysis and change if child sexual abuse is to be prevented. The datum clearly suggests that a reasonable approach to prevention lies in the resocialization and reeducation of males. Second, prepubertal children are at the greatest risk for victimization. Again, this datum implies the early education and empowering of children to resist sexual assaults originating both outside and inside of the family is a necessary step towards prevention. Third, victims of child sexual abuse are not inclined to disclose their experiences to anyone. Their apparent willingness to keep secret an event that most subjectively experience as traumatic places the responsibility on adults and on society in general to be sensitive to the indicators of abuse; to create a trusting, caring environment conducive to disclosure; and to convey their willingness to serve as an advocate for the victim, as another means towards the prevention of child sexual abuse.

359. Finkelhor, D. **Sexually Victimized Children.** New York: The Free Press, 1979.

A survey with questions about childhood sexual experiences with adults and children, incestuous sexual experiences, and coercive sexual experiences at any age was administered to 796 New England college and university students. For the purpose of this survey incest is defined as sexual contact, including sexual intercourse, masturbation, hand-genital stimulation, oral contact, fondling, exhibitionism and sexual propositioning by a family member. Of the 530 female respondents, 1.3% had experienced incest with their father or stepfather. Most rate the experience as negative and data suggest that father-daughter incest has the most traumatic impact on the victim. A total of 28% of the female respondents report sexual encounters with family members. Of the 266 male respondents, 23% had sexual experiences with a family member. The mean age of victimization for girls is 10.2 years and 11.2 years for boys. The type of incest experienced by both males and females and the mean trauma score for each type is also documented. The trauma scores range from 1 to 5, with one indicating a positive experience and five a negative experience. Few of the respondents had reported the sexual abuse to anyone.

Partner	Males ($\bar{x}$ tr. score)		Females ($\bar{x}$ tr. score)	
Father	0		5	(4.8)
Stepfather	0		2	(4.5)
Mother	0		1	(3.0)
Brother	15	(2.4)	72	(3.2)
Sister	16	(3.1)	18	(2.9)
Uncle	1	(3.0)	16	(4.0)
Aunt	1	(no ans.)	0	
Grandfather	0		1	(4.0)
Cousin, male	9	(3.0)	48	(3.1)
Cousin, female	33	(2.4)	16	(2.4)
Brother-in-law	0		5	(4.0)

360. Gagnon, J.H. "Female Child Victims of Sexual Offenses." **Social Problems**, 13(2): 176-192, Fall 1965.

Twelve hundred college age females who are white and predominantly middle class and who had earlier responded to the Kinsey Group survey on sexual behavior, are questioned regarding their sexual experiences during childhood. A total of 26% of the respondents report having had at least one sexual contact with an adult male before the age of thirteen; the mean age for the respondents at the time of the incident was 9.9 years old. A total of 4.4% of the respondents had been incestuously abused by a family member and slightly less than 1% had been victimized by their father or stepfather. Males are the aggressors in 98.5% of all cases of childhood sexual abuse in this sample. The vast majority of the women assessed the experiences as negative in their impact on their psychological well-being.

361. Landis, C. **Sex in Development.** New York: Harper and Brothers, 1940.

A sample of 142 psychiatrically hospitalized female patients is compared to 153 nonhospitalized controls as to the nature and impact of early childhood sexual experiences. A total of 23.7% of the respondents from both groups had been sexually victimized before puberty, and 12.5%

from both groups had been incestuously victimized. More than half of the women describe the experience as unpleasant to extremely unpleasant.

362. Landis, J.T. "Experiences of 500 Children with Adult Sexual Deviation." **Psychiatric Quarterly** (Supplement), 30: 91-109, 1956.

A survey with questions about childhood sexual experiences was administered to 1495 college students. Of the 1028 female respondents, 35% had been sexually abused as a child by an adult; figures on those who had been incestuously victimized by a family member are not separated out from the larger statistic. The mean age at the time of the abuse was 11.7 years and in each case, the perpetrator was a male. Of the 467 male respondents, 30% report childhood sexual experiences with adults; again, the rate of incest is not separated out from that statistic. The mean age at the time of the abuse was 14.4 years for the males, and in 84% of the cases, the perpetrator was a male. The degree of trauma experienced is related to the type of sexual abuse reported, with intercourse and attempted intercourse rated as more traumatic than contact or exhibition; and to the degree of acquaintance between the child and perpetrator, with perpetrators known to the children creating more trauma than those who are strangers. Finally, the more serious the offense, the less likely the victim reported it to anyone.

363. Kinsey, A.C.; Pomeroy, W.B.; Morton, C.E.; and Gebhard, P.H. **Sexual Behavior in the Human Female.** Philadelphia: Saunders, 1953.

A sample of 4,441 young, white, middle class, urban, educated females is interviewed about sexual behavior and childhood sexual experiences. A total of 24% report sexual molestation before puberty at a mean age of 9.5 years. Family members were responsible for the sexual victimization in 5.5% of the cases, and 1% of the respondents had been incestuously abused by a father or stepfather. In each case of reported sexual encounter, the perpetrator was a male.

Other Statistical Studies

Other statistical studies found in the professional literature present data on the rate of occurrence, nature of the incest, and the effects on the victims who are seen or treated in various specialized programs throughout the country. A few statistical studies also attempt to calculate the nationwide rate of child sexual abuse by extrapolating from various sources of data.

364. Conte, J.R. and Berliner, L. "Sexual Abuse of Children: Implications for Practice." **Social Casework,** 62(10): 601-607, December 1981.

A sample of 583 sexually abused children seen over a twenty-one month period of time at the Sexual Assault Center at the Harborview Medical Center in Seattle, Washington, is analyzed. A total of 47% of the victims had been molested by a family member and most of the incidents of incest involved fondling, oral contact or masturbation. Slightly over one-half of the incidents involved some degree of physical coercion by the perpetrator. Due to the power of the perpertrators in the children's lives, most of the victims were too frightened to disclose the sexual abuse to anyone; in fact, only 16% of the children in the total sample told anyone within forty-eight hours of the incident. Data analysis and confirmation of the children's accounts dispute the popularly held stereotype that children frequently give false reports of sexual abuse, or that incidents of sexual abuse by adults are the products of the imagination of children.

365. Kahn, M. and Sexton, M. "Sexual Abuse in Young Children." **Clinical Pediatrics,** 22(5): 369-372, May 1983.

Over an eighteen month period of time, all cases of child sexual abuse treated at the Pediatric Outpatient Clinic at the University of Maryland School of Medicine, were referred to a social work team for analysis and the collection of data. A sample of 113 children below the age of twelve who had been referred shows that 44% had been incestuously abused by a family member. A variety of behavioral and emotional problems are documented for the victims who also have a high rate of venereal disease. The perpetrators of the abuse were males in 93% of the cases, and most of the victims are females. Speculations about biases that may preclude the identification of male child sexual abuse victims are also offered.

366. Kroth, J.A. **Child Sexual Abuse.** Springfield, Illinois: Charles C. Thomas, Publisher, 1979.

A thorough empirical analysis of the Child Sexual Abuse Treatment Program of Santa Clara County, California is offered, with special emphasis on the programs, treatment goals, training models, and the computerized data system.

367. Russell, D.E.H. "The Incidence and Prevalence of Intrafamilial and Extrafamilial Sexual Abuse of Female Children." **Child Abuse and Neglect,** 7(2): 133-146, 1983.

A random survey of 930 San Francisco women who were questioned by specially trained interviewers matched wherever possible to the age and ethnicity of the respondents, was conducted. Defining incest as sexual contact whether wanted or unwanted with a relative at least five years older, or unwanted sexual contact with any other relative, the results show that 16% of the respondents report incestuous abuse before the age of eighteen.

368. Sarafino, E.P. "An Estimate of Nationwide Incidence of Sexual Offenses Against Children." **Child Welfare,** 58(2): 127-134, February 1979.

Using reported data on child sexual abuse from the state of Connecticut and Washington, D.C., and from the cities of Brooklyn and Minneapolis, it is extrapolated that 336,200 sexual offenses against children under the age of sixteen are reported in the country each year. Acknowledging that the number of unreported assaults is three to four times higher than the reported assaults, extrapolation would project a total of a million to 1.3 million cases per year. Reported data show that 92% of the cases are heterosexual in nature. Data also show that a standardized reporting system should be implemented throughout the country.

369. Shamroy, J.A. "A Perspective on Childhood Sexual Abuse." **Social Work,** 25(2): 128-131, March 1980.

A total of seventy-eight children under the age of thirteen was treated for child sexual abuse at the Children's Hospital Medical Center in Cincinnati in 1977. Analysis of the sample shows that sixteen of the children had been incestuously abused by a father or a stepfather, and that these children demonstrate the highest level of anxiety and ambivalence.

370. Swift, C. "Sexual Victimization of Children: An Urban Mental Health Survey." **Victomology: An International Journal,** 2(2): 322-326, 1977.

Thirty mental health clinicians were surveyed to determine their contact with child sexual abuse, which is defined for the purpose of this survey as rape; forced anal or oral intercourse; penetration of the oral, vaginal or anal orifice with an object; or molestation. The twenty respondents indicate that they have seen seventy-four cases of childhood sexual abuse over a designated twelve month period of time, and that those cases involve victimized children, adults reporting a childhood history of victimization, and the perpetrators of child sexual abuse. One-third of the victims are male, and in over one-half of the cases, the perpetrator was the natural father, stepfather or foster father of the victim. Male victims are more reticent to report than females, but all victims show a low rate of reporting.

12

Books and Literature Reviews

When S. Kirson Weinberg's scholarly treatise, **Incest Behavior,** was published in 1955, it was the first book in this country ever entirely devoted to an examination of incest. Its arrival was greeted with something less than enthusiasm by the sociologists and behavioral scientists who still preferred to relegate the study of incest to the quasi-scientific and titillating areas of erotic sex and perversion.

The thirty years since the publication of **Incest Behavior** have been kinder to researchers and theorists who have focused their attention on incest. Liberalized social and sexual attitudes and media coverage of this burgeoning social problem have created a milieu conducive to the study of incest, with the result that books varying from anecdotal accounts, to popularized presentations of research data written for the layperson, to texts for researchers and practitioners are being published with increasing regularity.

Chapters on incest are also found in books on child abuse and neglect, sexual dysfunction, family sociology, and abnormal behavior. Those references are not included in this chapter, however, which focuses on books dealing specifically with incest, and on those that address child sexual abuse in general but which also have detailed references to incest.

Anecdotal Accounts

The following references deal with incest on a very personal level. Most are written by adult survivors who share the story of their victimization and the incest-related problems they were forced to overcome.

371. Allen, C.V. **Daddy's Girl.** New York: Wyndham Books, 1980.

An autobiography of a survivor of ten years of paternal incest.

372. Armstrong, L. **Kiss Daddy Goodnight: A Speak-Out on Incest.** New York: Pocket Books, 1978.
First person accounts by victims of paternal incest are used to create an understanding of the nature of the incestuous family and the effects of incest on the victims.

373. Brady, K. **Father's Days: A True Story of Incest.** New York: Seaview Books, 1979.
The personal account of a ten year incestuous relationship between a daughter and her father.

374. Silverman, M.J. **Open and Shut.** New York: Bantam Books, 1981.
Written by a defense attorney, this is the true case of a woman who hired a contract killer to murder her husband after her daughter disclosed that he had incestuously victimized her.

Books for Professionals and Laypeople

The following books present research material in a manner that can be appreciated by both professionals in the field as well as laypeople who want to understand more about the dynamics and effects of incest.

375. Butler, S. **Conspiracy of Silence: The Trauma of Incest.** San Francisco: New Glide Publications, 1978.
Based upon hundreds of interviews with victims, perpetrators, and nonparticipating family members, this is an analysis of research illustrated with case studies.

376. Forward, S. and Buck, C. **Betrayal of Innocence: Incest and Its Devastation.** Los Angeles, California: J.P. Tarcher, Inc., 1978.
The case studies of twenty-five victims of incest are used to illustrate research on incest. Special attention is paid to the effects of incest on the victims.

377. Geiser, R.L. **Hidden Victims.** Boston, Massachusetts: Beacon Press, 1979.
All forms of child sexual abuse and sexual exploitation are examined.

378. Justice, B. and Justice, R. **The Broken Taboo.**
New York: Human Sciences Press, 1979.

The case histories of 112 incestuous families are used
to illustrate the dynamics of incest and its effects on the
victims.

379. Kempe, R.S. and Kempe, G.H. **The Common Secret:
Sexual Abuse of Children and Adolescents.** New York: W.H.
Freeman and Company, 1984.

Case examples are used to illustrate the dynamics
of incest and nonincestuous child molestation. Focus is also
placed on prevention and treatment.

380. Sanford, L.T. **The Silent Children: A Parent's
Guide to the Prevention of Child Sexual Abuse.** New York:
McGraw-Hill, 1980.

Written for parents and professionals, this book examines
the motives and circumstances of all types of sexual abuse
of children. Prevention and education are also stressed.

Books for Professionals

The following books are compilations of original research, in-depth examinations of research illustrated by
case examples, or theoretical considerations on the topic
of incest written for practitioners and researchers.

381. Barnard, C.P. (Editor). **Families, Incest and Therapy.**
New York: Human Sciences Press, 1984.

A blend of theory, pragmatic considerations, and case
illustrations is presented in this book which emphasizes
treatment techniques and modalities for incestuous families.

382. Burgess, A.W.; Groth, A.N.; Holmstrom, L.L.;
and Sgroi, S.M. **Sexual Assault of Children and Adolescents.**
Lexington, Massachusetts: Lexington Books, 1978.

A collection of articles on all aspects of child sexual
abuse with special focus on the dynamics and effects.

383. Conte, J.R. and Shore, D.A. **Social Work and Child
Sexual Abuse.** New York: Haworth Press, 1982.

A collection of articles covering the whole spectrum
of child sexual abuse with special emphasis on the treatment
of the victim, the family and the perpetrator.

384. De Francis, V. **Protecting the Child Victim of Sex Crimes Committed by Adults.** Denver, Colorado: American Human Association, 1969.

A comprehensive study of 523 cases of child sexual abuse, with focuses on the incidence, characteristics of the cases, the effects on the victims, and the community's response.

385. de Young, M. **The Sexual Victimization of Children.** Jefferson, N.C.: McFarland, 1982.

An empirical study of incest and nonincestuous child molestation, this book uses the case studies of eighty incest victims, sixty-nine perpetrators, and sixteen nonparticipating family members to illustrate the dynamics and effects of incest.

386. Finkelhor, D. **Sexually Victimized Children.** New York: The Free Press, 1979.

Results of a survey with questions about childhood sexual experiences with adults and children, incestuous sexual experiences, and coercive sexual experiences at any age which was administered to 796 New England college and university students, are presented. The literature is also reviewed to support the conclusions.

387. Fox, R. **The Red Lamp of Incest.** New York: E.P. Dutton, 1980.

This is an attempt to rewrite Freud's **Totem and Taboo** by pursuing a case history of the incest taboo from an anthropological perspective, using the theories of Darwin, Levi-Strauss, Freud and Marx.

388. Giaretto, H. **Integrated Treatment of Child Sexual Abuse.** Palo Alto, California: Science and Behavior Books, 1982.

The Child Sexual Abuse Treatment Program of Santa Clara County, California is described and the data on the more than 4,000 families treated there are presented.

389. Herman, J.L. **Father–Daughter Incest.** Cambridge, Massachusetts: Harvard University Press, 1981.

Forty victims of paternal incest are compared to a control group of twenty psychotherapy patients who do not report a history of incestuous victimization. A feminist analysis of their cases challenges traditional psychoanalytic theory that relegates accusations of incest victimization

to the fantasies of children; the male dominated social structure that has a vested interest in suppressing information
about the prevalence and effects of incest; and the legal
system that treats with skepticism any female who complains
of having been sexually victimized.

390. Kroth, J.A. **Child Sexual Abuse.** Springfield, Illinois:
Charles C. Thomas, Publisher, 1979.
    This is a thorough empirical analysis of the Child Sexual
Abuse Treatment Program of Santa Clara County, California,
with special emphasis on the programs, treatment goals,
training models, and the computerized data system.

391. Maisch, H. **Incest.** New York: Stein and Day, 1972.
    A West Germany sample of seventy-eight court-referred
cases of incest are examined, with special attention on the
dynamics of incest and the effects on the victims.

392. Masters, R.E.L. (Editor). **Patterns of Incest.** New
York: Julian Press, 1963.
    A series of articles on the dynamics and effects of
incest.

393. Mayer, A. **Incest: A Treatment Manual for Therapy
with Incest Victims, Spouses and Offenders.** Holmes Beach,
Florida: Learning Publications, Inc., 1983.
    This is a manual for therapists which describes the
treatment models and techniques for working with incest
victims, offenders, and with incestuous families.

394. Meiselman, K.C. **Incest: A Psychological Study
of Causes and Effects with Treatment Recommendations.**
San Francisco: Jossey-Bass, 1978.
    An empirical examination of fifty-eight cases of incest
in a psychotherapy sample, which are compared to a control
group of psychotherapy patients who do not report a history
of incest victimization. Special emphasis is placed on the
incest taboo, the dynamics of various types of incest, the
effects on the victim, and treatment.

395. Mrazek, P.B. and Kempe, C.H. **Sexually Abused
Children and Their Families.** Oxford, England: Pergamon
Press, 1981.
    A series of articles on child sexual abuse which cover
problems with definition, the law, psychodynamics of abuse,
treatment strategies and prevention.

396. Pincus, L. and Dare, C. **Secrets in the Family.** New York: Pantheon Books, 1978.

A psychodynamic approach to the unconscious beliefs, longings, and incestuous fantasies that shape family relationships.

397. Renshaw, D.C. **Incest: Understanding and Treatment.** Boston: Little, Brown and Company, 1982.

A descriptive approach to incest, this study focuses on the individual pathology of the members of the incestuous family. Cases are used to illustrate the dynamics.

398. Renvoize, J. **Incest: A Family Pattern.** London: Routledge and Kegan Paul, 1982.

Case examples are used to illustrate the research on incest.

399. Rush, F. **The Best Kept Secret.** Englewood Cliffs, New Jersey: Prentice Hall, 1980.

Social, religious and political patterns throughout history that have been conducive to the sexual victimization and sexual exploitation of children are analyzed from the feminist prospective.

400. Schultz, L.G. (Editor). **The Sexual Victimology of Youth.** Springfield, Illinois: Charles C. Thomas, Publisher, 1980.

A collection of articles covering the legal control of child sexual abuse, diagnosis and treatment, incest and the victim, and the justice system.

401. Thorman, G. **Incestuous Families.** Springfield, Illinois: Charles C. Thomas, Publisher, 1983.

An overview of the extent, nature and effects of incest with case illustrations.

402. Weinberg, S.K. **Incest Behavior.** New York: Citadel, 1955.

An analysis of 203 reported cases of incest with special focus on the dynamics of incest and the sociology of the family.

Literature Reviews

A review of the literature on incest reveals that the conclusions regarding its effects, the therapeutic modalities

required for treatment, and its prevention are largely dependent on the type of incest behavior, its frequency and duration,
the presence of threats and coercion, and the degree of
relatedness between the perpetrator and the victim. To
a considerably more subtle and certainly less measurable
effect, the conclusions of incest research are also dependent
on the biases of the researchers.

When these variables are manipulated, data from the
literature can be used to support various philosophical posi-
tions, as the following literature reviews demonstrate.

403. Bagley, C. "Childhood Sexuality and the Sexual
Abuse of Children: A Review of Treatment Strategies."
Clinical Psychology Review, 1: 211-222, 1981.

A review of the literature shows that family therapy
is most effective after the individual family members have
been treated; insight-oriented therapy is the only therapy
used for treatment of the longterm effects of incest for
the victim; and a multi-component treatment package for
the abuser and the victim, as well as combinations of interventions, are especially effective as treatment strategies.

404. Elwell, M.E. "Sexually Assaulted Children and
Their Families." **Social Casework,** 60(4): 227-235, April 1979.

A review of the literature on child sexual abuse, with
special emphasis on the variables in rate, definition and
effects.

405. Henderson, D.J. "Incest: A Synthesis of Data."
Canadian Psychiatric Association Journal, 17(4): 299-313,
1972.

A review of the literature suggests that incest is not
particularly common, that girls play a collusive role in their
victimization, and that the effects are not notably serious.

406. Koch, M. "Sexual Abuse in Children." **Adolescence,**
15(59): 643-648, Fall 1980.

A brief review of the literature on sexual abuse which
focuses on incest, supports a non-alarmist view about the
effects of incest on the victims.

407. Lystad, M.H. "Sexual Abuse in the Home: A Review
of the Literature." **International Journal of Family Psychiatry,**
3(1): 3-31, 1982.

This thorough literature review examines all kinds
of intrafamilial sexual abuse, from marital rape through

incest. Theoretical, statistical and causal studies are examined.

408. Mrazek, P.J. "Bibliography of Books on Child Sexual Abuse." **Child Abuse and Neglect,** 7(2): 247-249, 1983.

A list of forty-four books on the general topic of child sexual abuse, and a list of fourteen other books with chapters or selections pertinent to the topic.

409. Schultz, L.G. "The Sexual Abuse of Children and Minors: A Bibliography." **Child Welfare,** 58(3): 147-163, March 1979.

An extensive bibliography that is divided into sections on the history of child sexual abuse, sexual development in children, interviewing techniques with victimized children, sexual molestation, incest, sexual exploitation, rape, treatment, prevention, the law, and the courts.

410. Vander Mey, B.J. and Neff, R.L. "Adult-Child Incest: A Review of Research and Treatment." **Adolescence,** 17(68): 717-735, Winter 1982.

This comprehensive literature review highlights problems with definitions, reporting statistics, characteristics of the perpetrators and victims, the dynamics of the incestuous family, and effects of incest on the victim, treatment and prevention, and the legal requirements regarding reporting. Methodological problems in incest research are also examined.

13
Conclusion

A great deal is known about incest. Contrary to the laments of some researchers who insist that there is not enough data to constitute a scientific body of knowledge, or that incest research is redundant, rhetorically manipulative, or value-laden, the references included in this book demonstrate that there is a wealth of knowledge about incest in the professional literature and that the bulk of it is valid, communicable, and compelling.

It is true that a great deal of incest research is descriptive in nature and that it is not of the truly empirical quality that characterizes so much social science research. Good description is the beginning of science, however, and these studies on incest have provided a solid base of knowledge. Now the task of researchers and theorists committed to this topic is to build upon that base and to create a higher level of understanding about this behavior that has an impact on the lives of so many people.

Author Index

149

151 Author Index

Johnson, M.S. 29, 121
Julian, V. and Mohr, C.
4, 60
Justice, B. and Justice,
R. 30, 61, 79, 137,
214, 261, 378

Kahn, M. and Sexton, M. 365
Kaplan, S.L. and Kaplan,
S.J. 106, 297
Kaufman, I.; Peck, A.L.;
and Tagiuiri, C.K.
16, 80, 138
Keefe, M.L. 309
Kempe, R.S. and Kempe,
C.H. 379
Kinsey, A.C.; Pomeroy,
W.B.; Morton, C.E.;
and Gebhard, P.H. 363
Kirkland, K.D. and Bauer,
C.A. 62
Knittle, B.J. and Tuana,
S.J. 139, 346
Koch, M. 407
Kreiger, M.J.; Rosenfeld,
A.A.; Gordon, A.;
Bennett, M. 326
Kroth, J.A. 81, 353, 366, 390
Kubo, S. 5, 237, 247, 274

Labai, D. 316
LaBarbera, J.D. and Emmett,
D. 155
Landis, C. 361
Landis, J.T. 362
Langsley, D.G.; Schwartz,
M.N.; and Fairbairn,
R.N. 202
Lester, D. 227
Levin, S.M.; Barry, S.M.;
Gambaro, S.; Wolfin-
sohn, L.; and Smith,
A. 347
Levitan, H. 178

Lindzey, G. 228
Lukianowicz, N. 17, 82,
98, 248, 275
Lumsden, C.J. and Wilson,
E.O. 229
Lustig, N.; Dresser, J.W.;
Spellman, S.W.; Murray,
T.B. 31, 83
Lystad, M.H. 408

McCarthy, B. 327
McCarty, L.M. 310, 334
MacFarlane, K. and Bulkley,
J. 354
MacFarlane, K. and Korbin,
J. 32
McIntyre, K. 91
Machota, P.; Pittman,
F.S.; and Flomenhaft,
K. 33, 289
Magal, V. and Winnick,
H.Z. 18, 232, 249
Maisch, H. 19, 63, 84,
140, 148, 391
Malmquist, C.P.; Kiresuk,
T.J.; and Spano, R.M.
162
Masson, J.M. 107, 298
Masters, R.E.L. 392
Mayer, A. 327, 393
Medlicott, R.W. 141, 203,
220, 276, 281
Meiselman, K.C. 20, 73,
92, 142, 149, 169,
170, 182, 188, 189,
204, 221, 233, 238,
250, 253, 262, 267,
282, 288, 292, 394
Messer, A.A. 34
Miller, J.; Moeller, D.;
Kaufman, A.; DiVasto,
P.; Pathak, D.; and
Christy, J. 163
Molnar, G. and Cameron,
P. 150

Subject Index

Denial 12, 57, 77, 79, 80, 87, 92, 152
Depression 16, 121
Disclosures of Incest 19, 28, 97, 98, 101, 103, 104-111, 120,
    129, 131, 162, 195, 215, 236, 243, 295-306, 364
Displacement 57, 58, 59, 96, 109
Drawings of Victims 343
Dysuria 114

Eating Disorders 114, 119, 121, 122, 217, 329
Ecosystem Approach 339
Effects on Victims 15, 16, 51-53, 93-95
    on adolescents 132-155, 214-217
    on adults 156-197, 218-224
    on boys in father-son 209-224
    on boys in maternal incest 265-279
    on children 112-131, 209-213
    on girls in maternal incest 280-283
    on grandchildren 290-292
    on nephews 289
    on nieces 284-288
    on siblings 243-255
Encopresis 114
Endogamy 54, 59, 69, 73
Enuresis 114, 329
Eroticization of Victims 99, 131
Examination of Victims (Medical) 128, 311-313

Families, Paternally Incestuous:
    characterological perspective 10-22
    feminist perspective 40-46
    general perspective 47-54
    psychosocial perspective 23-39
    sociological perspective 4-9
Family Therapy 331-340
Father-Daughter Incest 4-111
Father Figures 183, 184
Father-Son Incest 198-224
Fathers, Incestuous 6, 7, 11, 12, 14, 15, 17, 18, 19, 20, 22,
    25, 55-75, 198-205, 230, 233
Feminism 40-46, 91
Fetishism 273
Feudal Family System 5
Filicide 160
Flashbacks 186